A modern inflatable liferaft for yachts and fishing vessels, accommodating four to eight persons. (Photo courtesy of SEACO/ELLIOT Inc., Riviera Beach, Florida.)

The Captain's Guide to Liferaft Survival

THE Captain's Guide TO Liferaft Survival

Captain
MICHAEL CARGAL
Master Mariner

SHERIDAN HOUSE

This book is dedicated to my brother,
Captain George Cargal,
who first took me out onto the sea.

ACKNOWLEDGEMENTS

I would like to thank

Dr. Terrance M. Davidson, Director of Continuing
Medical Education at the University of California
at San Diego, for reading and criticizing the
medical sections;
Alex Hickethier, President of the Southern California
Merchant Marine Training Services, for reading
and criticizing the navigation chapter; and
Muppy Haigler, RN, MS, for bringing me up to date on CPR.

Any errors which have crept in are my fault, not theirs.

Library of Congress Cataloging-in-Publication Data

Cargal, Michael, 1946–
    The Captain's guide to liferaft survival / Michael Cargal.
        p.   cm.
    ISBN 0-924486-00-7
        1. Survival (after airplane accidents, shipwrecks, etc.)—
Handbooks, manuals, etc.   2. Life rafts—Handbooks, manuals, etc.
I. Title.
VK1259.C37   1990
623.88'8—dc20   90-8206
                                                  CIP

Cover, design and illustrations by Jeremiah B. Lighter

Printed in the United States of America
ISBN 0-924486-00-7

CONTENTS

10 NAVIGATION 91

11 RESCUE 119

12 LANDFALL 121

13 MAKING A SURVIVAL KIT 135

APPENDICES
FORMULAS, ALMANAC, TABLES 151

INDEX 179

INTRODUCTION

Stephen Callahan learned in 1982 that odds of a million to one against something mean that every so often it happens to somebody. Callahan was sailing his 21-foot sloop across the Atlantic, asleep at night, alone in a thousand square miles of ocean, when a whale destroyed his boat in an instant. The whale was probably surfacing at a dead run from the bottom after feeding and had no idea the boat was there. Callahan grabbed his survival kit and some odd gear and spent 76 days alone on a raft in the Atlantic Ocean.

Every year vessels sink, burn, blow up, capsize, or get fatally rammed by whales, and their crews take to the liferafts. Sometimes they drift for months.

Liferafts certified for ocean service typically carry enough water and food for 3 to 7 days. The raft itself might be guaranteed only for 30 days. If you spend more than a few days in a liferaft, you will wish you had carried a few things with you, and you will wish to have done some preparation.

This book will tell you what you need to have and what you need to know to survive in a liferaft or lifeboat, short term and long term, and how to make the term as short as possible.

BEING CAPTAIN
OF A LIFERAFT

For you to be an effective leader in a liferaft, the crew must have confidence in your judgment, skill and fairness. I assume you are a good captain, but keeping people alive in a liferaft is not the same as running an operating vessel. You are still responsible for the well-being of your raft and crew, and some of the skills are the same, but the big problems are different, what you need to know is different, and your relationship with the crew is different.

KNOW WHAT TO DO

Being wrong in a liferaft can lead to someone's death, possibly your own. Both crewmembers and passengers sometimes do fatally foolish things in emergencies, because they panic or because they don't know any better. It is the captain's responsibility to know better and to tell people what to do. For example, if several people in lifejackets are floating near each other in cold water, you must know that they should huddle quietly together rather than exercise for warmth.

Since you already have this book in your hand, the quickest way to know what to do is to keep reading.

PREPARE AHEAD OF TIME

The likelihood of surviving in a life-vessel increases if you have done some preparation:
— Put together a survival kit (as described in Chapter 13), and secure it near a liferaft.
— Train your crew in launching a liferaft or lifeboat and getting into it.

MERCHANT VESSELS

On merchant vessels, preparation is prescribed by law. You must post a station bill which states everyone's responsibility in emergencies. In the case of abandoning ship, crewmembers should be assigned to:

— Muster and direct the passengers, making sure they are wearing lifejackets
— Gather blankets, portable radios and other useful items described in Chapter 2, "Abandoning Ship."
— Prepare and launch the rafts or boats

Every crewmember should be assigned to a particular raft or boat, with one person in charge. This should be a licensed deck officer, an able seaman or a certificated lifeboatman. Every raft commander should have a list of people in that raft and should make sure they know their duties when abandoning ship.

If you have lifeboats equipped with motors, people qualified to run them should be assigned to each boat. Also, if you have a radiotelegraph or a searchlight, someone who knows how to use it should be assigned to the lifeboat in which it is kept.

Training is not limited to explaining once what to do. Masters of merchant vessels are required to hold fire and boat drills at least once a week. If more than 25 percent of the crew is replaced, the master is required to hold a drill within 24 hours of leaving port.

CONFIDENCE AND STRESS

The most important psychological factor in surviving at sea is believing you can make it. Your role is to make everyone believe it.

The best way to minimize stress is for those involved to understand the situation and believe they have some control over what happens. As near as you can guess, tell them what they will face and what they can do to overcome it. Let them know the range of possible outcomes, from the best to the worst.

As captain of a liferaft, you are responsible for the occupants. But you cannot save them by yourself. They must believe there is something they can do which will affect whether they live or die. They must believe that their sacrifice and participation are important to the survival of the group.

DISCUSS YOUR OPTIONS

In a liferaft, you need to consult with the crew about decisions. They need to understand what is going on around them, and to believe they have a part in it.

Discussing options does *not* mean putting everything to a vote. You must remain captain. You must make the decisions, but explain the choices you have, and invite comments. If you decide to rig a sail and head 600 miles downwind toward rain rather than try to paddle 50 miles upwind toward land, explain to the crew why it's the right thing to do. Explain the currents, the relative speeds, and the cause-and-effect relationships among paddling, sweating, and drinking water.

It is not necessary for them to understand wind patterns. It is essential that they believe you understand them and that your decision is based on knowledge and experience and, therefore, likely to be the correct one. But if somebody else has a better idea, listen to it.

Do not hold anything back. Do not sugar-coat the situation. It is better for people to know the gravity of their position than for them suddenly to discover it and believe you have lied to them. If you want them to believe you later on, when you tell them they will die if they drink sea water, then you must not lie to them about anything.

On the other hand, they have to believe that survival is possible, so you must stay as confident as the situation will allow and try to build their confidence, too.

DISCIPLINE AND FAIRNESS

Discipline is important on a liferaft. You cannot have the nightwatch sneaking water or food.

In maintaining discipline, unity of will is more effective than chain of command. People will withstand hardship better if they believe their sacrifice is the right thing to do as part of the group than they will on the captain's or anybody else's orders. For castaways to be unified, everyone must feel a part of the group. There must be no factions and no outsiders. Everyone must feel fairly treated in the resolution of disputes and in the allocation of food, water, and work.

All of this is the responsibility of the captain. You must be open and fair all the time, stressing the survival of the group.

DIVIDING FOOD

If you must divide something that does not come in uniform pieces (such as a cut-up fish), there are two fair ways to decide who gets which piece. If there are only two people, one can divide the food as evenly as possible while the other chooses his portion. With three people, the choosers can alternate picking first.

If there are more of you, first divide the food as evenly as possible and then have one person turn away. Someone else points to a portion at random and asks, "Whose is this?" The person whose back is turned says a name. Repeat until the food is distributed. This is a very old method of distributing food. Captain Bligh used it in the lifeboat after the mutiny on *H.M.S. Bounty*.

If you must make exceptions, such as giving extra water to drowning victims, explain about flushing salts from the body. It is not as important that they understand the explanation as it is that they believe there is a reason other than favoritism for the unequal rations.

Do not wait until somebody asks. Many crewmembers will not question the captain out loud, and a misunderstanding about unequal rations could fester into mutiny.

OCCUPYING TIME NONVIOLENTLY

If you spend a few weeks in a liferaft, there will be a great deal of time with nothing to do after everything pleasant has been said. This can degenerate into bickering and fighting.

Try to fill some of this time with activity. Make individuals responsible for particular duties such as medical care, raft maintenance, rationing, navigation, or sailing.

You can make a production out of finding and charting your position twice a day. Most crews have one or two interested in learning navigation. There is no better way of occupying time than in learning how to find out where you are. You might read from this book aloud for half an hour twice a day, to refresh everyone's memory.

Talking about food is popular on liferafts. People will talk for hours about what they would like to eat, or meals they will serve in the restaurant they plan to buy when they get home, or what would be the finest meal in the world. This is healthy and gets everyone involved.

Fishing is a most worthwhile recreation, both practical and absorbing.

LOGS

Do your best to salvage the ship's log, and maintain it in the raft. If you cannot salvage it, begin a new log on whatever paper or other material you have available.

WATCHES

Watches should be set from the beginning, to avoid dangerous wreckage. Keep them short. Two hours is plenty to start with. One hour is enough after everyone is tired, weak, and dehydrated. If you have enough people, put two at a time on watch.

Because of the canopy over an inflatable liferaft, you cannot see anything unless you are sitting or standing in one of the entrances. Do not risk exposure. If the weather is cold, the watch will have to bundle up and stand or kneel wrapped up in the entry cowling, taking special care to protect the head. If it is hot, the watch should wear sunglasses, sunscreen, and hats. In very hot or very cold weather, watchstanders should spend most of their time inside the canopy and just look outside from time to time. Leave the hatches closed in cold weather.

But do maintain watches. You must not miss seeing a passing ship. Everyone needs to be roused in case of rain so you can catch the maximum amount. And somebody has to pump the watermaker or tend the still.

Watches also help maintain the structured relationship of a vessel's crew, which reduces tension and adds to your authority when you tell them you are sailing for the South American coast rather than the Galapagos, because it provides a bigger target.

PHANTOM SHIPS

Be prepared for arousal and disappointment. In the intense darkness of the empty ocean, watchstanders are more likely than usual to mistake Venus and Jupiter for a ship's mast lights.

SMOKING

Anyone who smokes must be very careful with matches and cigarettes or your raft might melt.

If the entrances are closed, smoke is liable to be offensive, especially to non-smokers, and should be prohibited. If they must smoke, let them stand watch for a while, keeping head and smoking materials outside.

When water is low, you should prohibit smoking, as it makes people thirstier than they otherwise would be.

MENTAL INSTABILITY

People sometimes go crazy on liferafts. This can be caused by fear, injury, exhaustion, or drinking sea water. Often it is mild, and all you have to do is humor them. Sometimes, it's serious. They might jump overboard and try to swim home. If someone seems seriously deranged, you may have to restrain them.

IGNORANT CAPTAINS

Do not let anyone die because the captain doesn't know what to do. If you are not the captain, and you hear the captain give advice or an order which is clearly wrong and could kill someone, speak up in a loud clear voice and explain why it is wrong.

For example, if a severely hypothermic person is brought aboard the raft, and the captain recommends rubbing the wrists because the blood comes closest there, you should point out that rubbing the wrists could kill the person because it draws more heat away from internal organs.

If you are the captain, and somebody tells you that you have made a serious mistake, think about it. They might be right. Do not let anyone die because you did not know what to do and would not listen to someone who did.

ABANDONING SHIP

STAY CALM

The few minutes or seconds between deciding to abandon ship and actually going into the water are critical. At best, they will be hectic and scary, but what you do then may determine whether you and your crew survive. It's easy for me to sit at my desk and tell you to stay calm, but it is important, especially for the captain. Passengers and crew often base their perceptions of danger on how the captain acts.

PRACTICE MAKES PERFECT

Whatever you're like on the inside, you are much more likely to look calm on the outside and do the right things if you have thought about what to do and have practiced it. In those few crucial moments you will have to give orders for supplying and launching the liferaft. This requires really being in command.

If you are the captain of a pleasure yacht, prepare yourself. You might get some help from passengers and friends, but you cannot count on it. Before embarking on a long ocean cruise on a yacht, make sure everyone on board knows what to do in an emergency.

MERCHANT MARINE SIGNALS

On larger commercial vessels, the entire ship's company must be familiar with the standard Merchant Marine signals regarding liferafts and boats. When possible, the signals are delivered by the ship's whistle, followed by the same signal on the general alarm:
 — Six short blasts followed by one long blast: man lifeboat stations
 — One short blast: lower all boats
 — Two short blasts: stop lowering boats
 — Three short blasts: dismissed from boat stations

EAT AND DRINK NOTHING, ESPECIALLY NO ALCOHOL

If you have to jump into cold water, the sudden change in temperature can cause stomach cramps. This is not only painful and dangerous, it makes it much harder to swim to the raft and climb aboard. The presence of food or drink in the stomach increases the likelihood of cramps. Put food in plastic bags. You will need it later.

Heat loss causes most deaths that occur while abandoning ship. Alcohol raises body temperature, which causes you to lose heat faster. Alcohol also impairs judgment. You cannot afford that now.

DRESS WARM

If you have survival suits, use them. If you don't, wear several layers of warm clothes. This will help insulate you against the cold by reducing water circulation next to your skin. Besides, you will need the clothes later and it's easier to wear them than to carry them.

If you can, make the outside layer waterproof. A windbreaker with snug-fitting wrist elastic minimizes the flow of water inside it. Less water flow means less heat loss.

If you have something with a hood, wear it. Body heat dissipates very quickly through the top of the head.

WEAR A LIFEJACKET

Even if you are a strong swimmer, you must wear a lifejacket in the water. Your body will cool 35 per cent faster if you tread water than if you are wearing a lifejacket and can stay still in the water. Strap the jacket tight so it will not come off if you have to jump into the water. The only time not to wear a lifejacket is when you are already wearing a buoyant survival suit.

TAKE THE SURVIVAL KIT

And take anything that's handy, especially:
- — Food and water
- — Personal medicine
- — Eyeglasses
- — Navigation gear
- — Emergency Position-Indicating Radio Beacon (EPIRB)
- — Hand-held VHF radio
- — Blankets

Take all the food and water you have time to get. Put the food in plastic bags to keep it dry.

You will have a better chance of survival if you know where you are, so take navigation gear: charts, sextant, tables, watch, Nautical Almanac, protractor, dividers, pencil and paper.

A portable radio will help pass the time. Some small ones can get single-sideband, so you can listen on a distress frequency (2182 KHz) to hear if anyone has heard your mayday and relayed it. You can follow your rescue by radio.

If the boat has a dinghy, cut it loose and tow it behind the raft. Rafts are not guaranteed for as long as you might be adrift.

Spare canvas or sheet plastic might become a sail.

Lines are always useful.

Sailboaters should take the man-overboard pole. It might have several uses, including holding up a radar reflector or serving as a jury-rigged mast.

LAUNCHING THE RAFT

First release the raft from its cradle. On inspected vessels, kick the button on the hydrostatic release, the aluminum catch shown in the picture. If your vessel is not inspected, familiarize yourself with how to release the raft.

To release the canister from its cradle, kick the hydrostatic release button at the arrow.

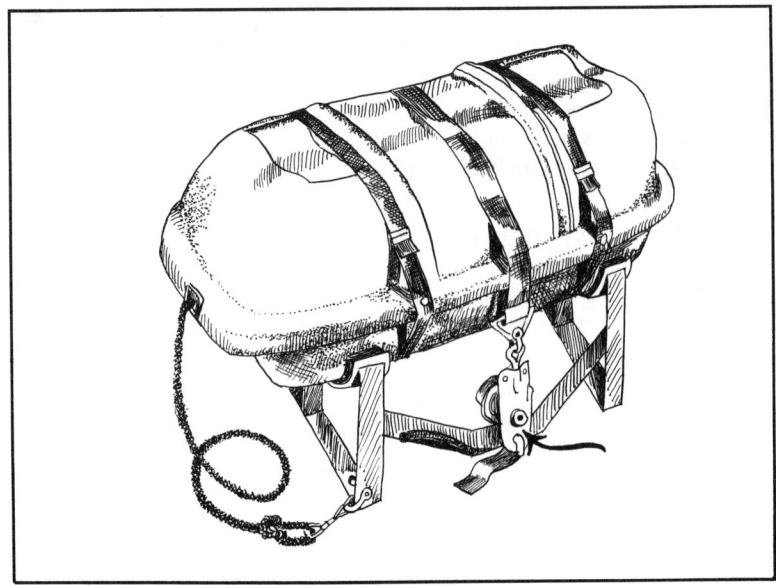

Throw the raft overboard, on the downwind side if possible. Pull the line coming out of the canister. When it reaches its limits, give it a sharp jerk. This will trigger the CO_2 cartridge and inflate the raft.

Inflating the Raft on Deck is Dangerous

I have heard of people inflating their raft on deck or on the cabin and floating it off when their boat sank from under them. Do this only as a last resort. It is extremely dangerous in several ways:

— Unless the raft is the kind kept in a valise, the canister explodes open. In some brands, the two halves and stainless steel straps go flying. If you must inflate the raft on deck, turn your back when you pull the cord.
— While inflating, the raft can become jammed between the bulwarks and the cabin or between the mast and the rigging.
— If the vessel rolls over, the raft can catch in the rigging or be slashed by barnacles.
— If the sinking vessel is large, the suction when it goes down will not sink the raft but it might swamp you. The turbulence can make it impossible to get in or stay in the raft.

One liferaft company (Givens) does claim its raft can be inflated on deck. I still would not try it.

Automatic Release

If you cannot release the raft from its cradle, those with hydrostatic releases will be released automatically as soon as the vessel reaches a certain depth, usually ten to 15 feet. The canister will float to the surface, and when the vessel sinks to the end of the painter, the raft will inflate automatically. The weak link, where the painter is attached to the cradle, will break. But do *not* count on all this. Even if the raft is released from its cradle, it can still hang up on the superstructure or rigging. It is smaller and less buoyant before inflation, and more likely to foul.

LEAVING THE VESSEL

The captain should be the last to leave the vessel. This is another reason to hold abandon-ship drills.

If possible, go straight from the sinking vessel into the raft, to stay dry. You can get into the raft before it is fully inflated.

One liferaft company (Elliot) says that if the distance is 15 feet or less, you can jump onto the top of its raft after it is inflated and then tumble in at the entrance. Another company (Viking) specifically warns against it, for fear of hurting yourself or someone already in the raft.

If you must enter cold water, try to ease in. Jumping in can shock you into gasping underwater. Breathing sea water is unpleasant at best. At worst, it is fatal.

If you must jump in, do it feet first. Hold your nose with one hand and your lifejacket with the other, so it cannot ride up around your head when you hit the water.

Try to land vertically. Water is hard when you jump into it from any height, and there may be debris in it, which you would rather hit feet-first. If you hit the water or debris in a sitting position, you can fracture a vertebra or injure your kidneys. If you land flat, your lungs and kidneys are at risk. If you dive head first, you can injure your head or neck even if there is no debris, because your lifejacket will change your trajectory when you hit the water.

You might be able to jump into a swimming pool in any of these ways, but it is different going into a rough sea with debris all around, wearing clothes and a lifejacket. On top of that, it may be dark and you will certainly be anxious. Do not take chances. Jump feet first.

If you have to jump into burning oil, swim upwind. If you swim downwind, the oil will travel with you. Use the breast stroke to push the flames away from your head.

When the raft is fully inflated, you will hear a loud hissing. That is the relief valve. It is normal and it will soon stop.

Once in a while, a raft will inflate upside down. In that case, go to the downwind side of the raft and face into the wind. Grab the straps crossing the bottom. Get your knees up on the edge of the raft, or stand on it, then pull and lean back. It should tip easily once the wind catches it. If there is no wind, find the side which has the inflation cylinder and follow the same procedure.

STAY WARM AND SAVE ENERGY

Get into the raft as quickly as possible. Cold water sucks heat from you faster than cold air, so it is essential that you minimize the time and effort spent battling seawater. Do not swim any farther than you have to. And don't swim just to get warm. Not only does it use energy, but the increased water circulation around you actually draws heat away from you faster.

Exposure to cold water can very quickly rob you of feeling and agility in your extremities. So, if you have to float for a while, put the whistle from your lifejacket in your mouth while you still have enough dexterity to do it.

If you are wearing a lifejacket, float quietly and reduce the surface area you expose to the water. Fold your arms across your chest and hold your legs together to save heat. Try to get your hands into your armpits for warmth.

If there is large flotsam around, hold on to it and pull yourself as far out of the water as possible.

If you're wearing a survival suit, float with your feet into the wind. Otherwise, face downwind. If you are still getting water in your face, cup your hands over your face and breathe through your fingers.

If two or three of you have to wait to get into the raft, huddle together as if you are dancing. This is not the most efficient method for saving heat, but it's easy to do and it's a lot better than floating alone.

There is a technique for saving energy while floating in warm water called "drownproofing." This involves letting your head go under the water between breaths. If you find yourself in cold water without a lifejacket, don't try it. You will lose much more heat through your head than you will use treading water.

Remember: Stay calm; conserve body heat; do not waste energy. You will need it later.

Righting an overturned raft.

THE FIRST FEW MINUTES IN THE RAFT

The first person into the raft should throw the heaving line to others, so they will not have to swim. The heaving line has a rubber donut (a quoit) on the end. If necessary, you can put it on your arm and swim to them.

CAPTAIN TAKE CHARGE

The first thing the captain should do after entering the raft is take command. This does not mean shouting, "I'm in command here." Establish command by taking charge, by telling people what to do as though you had the right, which you do. Just continue to be captain in the raft.

If the captain is dead or missing, the senior officer should take charge.

If there are several rafts, make sure there is an officer or senior crewmember in each one. As soon as immediate rescue operations are over, re-establish the previous line of command. Everyone on every raft should know who is in charge.

The next several steps are listed in order of importance, but if you have several people in a raft, they each can be doing different things at the same time. For example, while two survivors are hauling others aboard, another one can be providing first aid while someone else bails out the raft.

GET EVERYBODY OUT OF THE WATER

The colder the water, the more important it is to get out of it quickly. Your first medical concern is hypothermia, extreme loss of body heat. This can happen anywhere, since every ocean is cooler than human body temperature. Furthermore, survivors in the water are certainly anxious and probably panicky. They will swim less efficiently and lose more heat than they might on a Sunday swim in the same waters.

CUT LOOSE FROM THE SINKING VESSEL

When a vessel sinks, you do not want to be attached to it. The danger is not that you'll be pulled under, but if the vessel rolls over, a wave can swamp you or barnacles on the hull can slice the raft. You do not want to be directly above it, either. Surfacing debris might hit the raft.

If the vessel is burning or going down, paddle away from it. One raft-maker (Elliot) recommends that you cut the automatic sea-anchor loose, paddle away, and then deploy the spare sea anchor. Many rafts do not have a spare, so make sure your raft does before you cut your sea anchor loose. In any case, a sea anchor takes a little while to get to the end of its rode, so be prepared to paddle some distance before it takes effect.

If the abandoned vessel stays afloat, stay near it if you can. You may be able to salvage some equipment from it, or food and water. Even a capsized hulk is likely to be easier for rescuers to see than a liferaft. It's bigger, which also makes it a better radar target. If you were able to get out a mayday call, rescuers will start their search at the position you broadcast. A vessel awash is a big sea anchor. The wreck will probably stay nearer where you abandoned it than a liferaft alone would.

If the abandoned vessel is small, you can tie onto it. Do not tie on too firmly. Use a slip-knot or loop the line around something and hold on to the end. Be alert. If the boat starts to sink, let go or cut the line. You do not want to go down with the ship after making it this far.

If you are in a lifeboat rather than a liferaft, keep your craft at right angles to the ship. If you are not perpendicular to it you stand a chance of being beaten against it. If you are bow on, you can back off easier and will suffer less damage if you do hit the hulk.

DEPLOY THE SEA ANCHOR

Stream the sea anchor as soon as you are away from the vessel. This will keep the raft from tipping over in rough seas and give you a more stable platform on which to perform first aid. It also minimizes seasickness and consequent dehydration.

With some rafts, deployment is automatic. In others, it will be in the center of the raft floor, ready for streaming overboard. In others, it will be in the raft's equipment bag, which is usually orange.

TREAT SERIOUS INJURIES AND SHOCK

Bleeding

Serious bleeding can kill very quickly. Stop it by applying pressure. Pressing a piece of folded cloth against the wound usually works best. A shirt will work fine. Press hard and keep pressing until the bleeding stops.

If the blood is squirting or pulsating, you may have to stick a finger or thumb into the wound to press down on the artery.

Drowning

Do not try to drain water from the lungs of a drowning victim. It does not help and it can hurt.

Water in the stomach is different. Drowning victims often swallow a lot of water, which can make it hard to breathe.

Drowning victims are often hypothermic. Warm them up. And give them extra water rations as soon as they are able to drink, to avoid dehydration.

People who nearly drown usually recover by themselves, but if a victim is unconscious and has no heartbeat or is not breathing, apply CPR (Cardio-Pulmonary Resuscitation).

CPR (Cardio-Pulmonary Resuscitation)

Start CPR immediately. You have only four to six minutes to prevent brain damage from the time the heartbeat and breathing stop.

Ordinarily a non-physician should stop giving CPR only when the victim has recovered, assistance arrives, a physician pronounces the victim dead, or you become exhausted and unable to continue. In a liferaft the captain must make the physician's judgment and decide when it is useless to continue. Don't give up too soon.

Cold-water Diving-reflex

If the water is very cold, victims can go into shock quickly. Breathing and heartbeat stop but they do not die right away. Children especially have spent half an hour or more underwater and revived. Administer CPR to anyone recovered from the sea cold and apparently dead. Administer CPR even if the water is as warm as 70° and the person has been in the water 30 minutes. Do not give up until the body has warmed up and still shows no sign of life.

Summary of CPR Steps

1. Lay the victim down face-up.
2. To open the airway, pull the chin forward by holding the angles of the victim's lower jaw and lifting with both hands. This is the safest means of opening the airway if there may be a neck injury.
3. If not breathing, hold the victim's nose and exhale two full breaths deeply into the patient's mouth. The chest should rise and fall. if it does not, tilt the victim's head back a little by pushing back on the forehead and check to see if anything is blocking the throat.
4. Check the pulse at the carotid artery in the groove in the neck created by the trachea and the large strap muscles of the neck. It will take five or ten seconds to find a pulse.
   If there is a pulse: Continue rescue breathing at a rate of twelve breaths a minute, or one every five seconds.
   If there is no pulse: Start compressing the heart. Depress the lower part of the sternum (breast bone) 1½ to 2 inches. Push down 80 to 100 times a minute.
   Check the carotid pulse again after one minute and then every five minutes. If you feel a pulse, stop compressing the heart.
6. Check the eyes from time to time. If the pupils contract when exposed to light, the brain is getting blood and oxygen.
7. If you are giving CPR by yourself, administer fifteen compressions at a rate of 80-100 per minute, then give two breaths.
   If you have help, at the end of the two breaths, verify the lack of pulse and breathing for 5 seconds. Then give two deep breaths and continue on the 15:2 cycle.

This is just a brief summary. American Merchant Marine officers are required to know CPR to obtain or renew a license. If you haven't taken a course in CPR, do so as soon as you can. It is worth going out of your way to learn.

Shock

Shock can occur as the result of a broken bone, loss of blood, inadequate blood circulation, or lack of oxygen, among other causes.

The skin of a person in shock is usually pale, cool, and damp. (If the victim has dark skin, examine the skin under the fingernails.) Breathing is rapid and shallow. The pulse is weak and fast, over 100. The victim may feel faint and often will be nauseated.

Shock Treatment:

— Have victims lie down with feet higher than the head. Prop feet up on the side of the raft.

— Keep them warm. Shock and hypothermia victims get first call on the blankets.

— If there is no wound to the head or stomach, you can give a shock victim water. If possible, add half a teaspoon of salt and a quarter of a teaspoon of baking soda per pint. Do not give liquids to anyone with an abdominal or head injury.

— Never give a shock victim alcohol in any form.

Hypothermia

Hypothermia is common among people who are pulled from cold water. Most people who die soon after getting into a liferaft are victims of acute hypothermia. They have been too cold for too long. Victims are typically pale and often rigid from tight muscles. The breath may smell like acetone, because of low blood sugar. They may be in shock and will probably be shivering. Shivering is a good sign. If a victim is not shivering, the body's heat-producing systems have broken down. If you have several victims to treat, first take care of the ones who are very cold but not shivering.

Treatment for Hypothermia:

— Try to keep victims horizontal when you pull them out of the water. Vertical lifting can cause heart failure.

— Warm them up fast. Take off all wet clothing. They should not have to use what little body heat they have left to warm wet clothes. Do this as gently as possible. Do not rub or massage them or handle them roughly. This draws blood and heat away from vital organs and can kill someone on the edge. For the same reason, arms and legs must not be warmed before the torso and head.

— Wrap them in plastic or blankets or clothing. Cover the head, but leave the face uncovered. If you have both sheet plastic and blankets, put the plastic on the inside. Do not put cold, dry clothes on them. Hypothermics do not have enough heat to heat up even dry clothes. Pre-warm the clothes if you can inside someone else's clothes, or have someone give their warm clothes to the victim.

— If victims are very cold or unconscious from the cold, have others get under the blankets with them, to share body heat.

— If you have no blankets or dry clothing, have one or two people take off their clothes and huddle close to a victim, concentrating on warming the torso and head rather than the arms and legs. Rotate these people often. Otherwise you run the risk of making others hypothermic.

— Keep a close watch on the victims as they recover. There is a risk of cardiac arrest as the body warms up. If the heart stops, immediately hit the victim hard in the middle of the chest. If that doesn't work, perform CPR.

— Do not give someone recovering from acute hypothermia anything by mouth for 24 hours, unless you have something sweet to drink, to build blood sugar. This especially means no alcohol or tobacco.

Broken Bones

Immobilize fractures. If you have nothing you can use for a splint, strap the broken part to the opposite side. Strap a broken leg to the good leg. A broken upper arm can be strapped to the chest. A broken forearm can be strapped across the chest or to the opposite forearm in front of the chest.

Duct tape works well for strapping broken bones, but be sure to pull if off the roll by hand and not by pulling against the injury. Wrap cloth or paper underneath the tape, so it doesn't stick to the skin. And don't make it tight enough to hinder circulation.

Burns

For minor (first degree) burns, apply cold fresh water. *Do not* use salt water. If the burned area is dirty, wash it gently with soap and water, if you have it. Leave it open to the air or cover it with a clean dry bandage.

For moderate (second degree) burns, apply cold fresh water, *not salt water*. Then clean the area with soap and water and blot dry with a clean cloth. If bits of flesh are stuck to the wound, leave them there. *Do not break blisters.*

If you have it, apply one percent sulfadiazine silver cream, and cover the area with a sterile dressing. Change the dressing daily, or more often if it soaks up a lot of exudate or starts to smell. Do not pull the dressing off; soak it off with fresh water.

There is not much you can do on a liferaft for severe (third degree) or extensive burns. Be prepared to give CPR.

Pain

Give aspirin or acetaminophen (Tylenol®) for pain. For severe pain, give morphine sulfate by injection. CAUTION: Morphine is a respiratory depressant. Do not give it to anyone who is hypothermic, frost-bitten, or whose breathing is for any reason not normal.

Prevent Exposure

Make sure everybody is warm and dry. You should be able to warm a covered raft to a comfortable temperature with body heat alone.

In all but the hottest weather, pump up the raft floor for insulation.

Bail and sponge the raft dry. Water in the bottom of a raft sucks heat from you faster than the air in the raft. The raft's equipment bag should have a bailer and one or two sponges. Your own survival kit should have some, too.

If it's cold, close the hatches, especially on the weather side. But watch out for carbon-dioxide buildup. Leave enough of an opening to allow ventilation. If it's hot, open everything up to get a breeze.

Wring out wet clothing or change into dry. Wool is best. It keeps you warm, but allows the air to circulate.

Take off your shoes; they restrict blood circulation. Pull your socks halfway off, so your toes are at the heel of the sock. This decreases air circulation around the toes.

Put a blanket on the raft floor, under everyone. If you are short on blankets, one underneath you will keep you warmer than one over you.

Wrap up in blankets. Space blankets on top of regular blankets are best, but use what you have. Two people under one blanket will be warmer than the same people with separate blankets. Lie in opposite directions, with each person warming the other's feet inside their clothes.

Spread a blanket or a sheet of plastic over the top of everyone, so you don't have to heat the whole raft with your bodies.

Prevent Seasickness

Anyone susceptible should be given seasickness pills to prevent dehydration.

Other Medical Problems

Put off other medical problems until you call for help. (Continuing medical care is discussed in chapter 8.)

TAKE INVENTORY

Find out what you have to work with. If you have an extensive survival kit, look just far enough to find a way to call for help. Do a full inventory later.

TURN OFF THE LIGHTS WHEN YOU DON'T NEED THEM

The raft's batteries have a life of twelve to 24 hours. Turn lights off in the daytime. Turn the interior light off at night when you're not using it. Some rafts have switches. On others, you will have to unscrew the inside bulb and disconnect the battery cable for the outside light.

GETTING HELP

Once injuries have been treated and everyone is as warm and dry as possible, you need to attract attention so you will be picked up. How you do this will depend on the contents of your survival kit. (For a full discussion of this kit and its contents, see Chapter 13.)

VHF RADIO

This is by far the easiest and fastest way to make contact. Most international shipping regularly monitors the distress channel, 16.

— Pre-call preparation:
  — Make sure the antenna is attached. Turn the radio on. Turn it to channel 16.
  — Stand up to call. You will extend your line-of-sight range by a mile or two.
— Making the call:
  — Hold the button down and begin the message:
    — Slowly say, "Mayday, Mayday, Mayday."
    — State your vessel's name and call sign three times.
    — Tell what kind of vessel you are. How long, what color, etc. Keep it simple. For example:
      — 64-foot motor yacht, all white
      — 186-foot supply boat, blue with white top
      — 46-foot sailboat, yellow with white sails
      — 650-foot container ship, gray with red stack.
    — State what happened: burned, sank, hit a reef, etc.
    — Give your position. First give range and bearing to a commonly known place; then give your latitude and longitude. Repeat.

— State how many people are with you. Any women or children?
— Are you still on board? In a raft?
— Are there any sick or injured?
— Do you have food and water?
— Are you in immediate danger?
— State the weather situation.
— Clarity counts:
  — Speak slowly. Now, of all times, you want to be understood.
  — Do not shout. Radios are electronic, not mechanical. They work best if you talk at a normal level.
— Go through the whole routine without stopping.
  — Just because you don't hear them does not mean they don't hear you.
  — Make sure you keep the transmitter button depressed throughout the message.
— Follow-up:
  — Stop talking; release the button and listen.
  — If nobody responds, wait five minutes and repeat the same routine. Keep the radio turned on in the meantime. Receiving does not require much power.
  — If nobody answers you the second time, wait half an hour and try again.
  — If nobody answers you the third time, try again after an hour.
  — You can try again from time to time, but there soon will come a time when you should save the battery and wait until you see a vessel before calling again.

EPIRB (EMERGENCY POSITION-INDICATING RADIO BEACON)

Your EPIRB is one of your most important pieces of rescue–related equipment. It will broadcast your position unattended night and day, foul-weather or fair, in sickness and in health. On an inspected vessel, the EPIRB is an orange plastic cylinder about four inches in diameter and 18 inches long, with a foot-long antenna. It is designed to float antenna-up in the water. You can tie the string that comes with it to the life-line around the raft. Usually all you have to do to turn it on is turn the unit antenna-side up, although some yacht-sized EPIRBs have to be switched on. You should be familiar with your own equipment.

Once you have turned it on, leave it on. Do not try to save the batteries by letting it transmit for only a few minutes at a time. To work right, it must broadcast continuously. All ships and cross-ocean planes are supposed to monitor the EPIRB frequency. Several satellites have been placed in orbit for just this purpose as part of the SARSAT program.

PYROTECHNICS

Your raft is equipped with a few flares and possibly some parachute flares. (Your survival kit should have some, too.) If you have a lot of them, and you are in a shipping lane, it might make you feel better to waste a parachute flare right away. In general, though, do not use a flare unless you sight a vessel. And don't fire off all your flares at the first ship you see. You may need them later. Many survivors tell of shooting off flares directly in a ship's path and still not being seen.

In the daytime, use your signal mirror first. Then light the flares after you have attracted attention. This will direct them to the spot.

To light a flare, pull the tape, pull off the cap, turn it around, and rub the rough surface sharply against the igniter button.

Remember that your raft is made of rubber. It will melt if you touch it with the flame of a flare. Light flares on the downwind side of the raft, and hold them out over the water. Rocket flares shoot fire out of both ends when you set them off. Make sure neither end is pointed at the raft. Hold them upright.

If you have flares of different colors, red is the proper color for distress signals.

DYE MARKER

This is designed to be seen by airplanes. It will not do much good at night, because they won't be able to see it; or in rough weather, because it will dissipate; or if you don't have a sea anchor, because the wind will push you away from it.

Despite the negatives, a dye marker can be seen in the daytime in moderate weather. If you are near a populated coast, go ahead and use it. If you are in mid—ocean, save it until you either see a plane or reckon you are beneath a flight path.

RADAR REFLECTOR

This is a most useful device. Rubber rafts and people do not reflect radar waves worth a darn, but radar reflectors do.

The purpose of a radar reflector is not just to bring you to someone's attention. It will do two things for you. First it will keep a ship from running right over you. They will think you're an iceberg or a net marker and will go around you, or at least be on the lookout. Second, if you can get the ship's attention with a flare or signal mirror, it will tell them just where you are. If the watch sees a flare, they might think it was a meteor. If the radar shows a target there, too, you are more likely to get picked up.

Mount the reflector as high as you can. If it is seven feet above the water, it will be seen from about a mile and a half farther away than if it is up only four feet. If you managed to save the man-overboard pole, use it as a mast to support the reflector. Otherwise tie it to the top of the raft.

If you sight a ship, you might even tie it to a paddle and hold it as high as you can. This is not so much to increase the distance that you can be seen, because if you can see the ship, its radar has a direct shot at you. But it will help to give a more consistent radar return to the ship at any distance by being visible to the radar on every sweep. If the reflector is too low, it will not be seen when the raft is in the troughs of the waves, so the radar can miss the reflector for a sweep or two. Constant reflection from one spot shows up as a target. The higher the reflector, the better you will stand out from the sea clutter.

SIGNAL MIRROR

This is a mirror a few inches in diameter which is reflective on both sides and has a hole in the middle. To use it to signal a plane or ship, first reflect sunlight onto a nearby surface, to make sure it is reflecting generally in the right direction.

Then raise the mirror to a few inches in front of your face, and look through the hole in the middle until you see the plane or ship.

Some sunlight will come through the hole and land on your face or shirt. You should be able to see the spot reflected in the back side of the mirror.

Tilt the mirror to make the reflection of the spot of light move over your hand or face until it disappears in the hole while you can still see the plane or ship. The reflection is now shining right on your target.

Do not blind the pilot. Once the plane or ship has changed course to come look for you, or has otherwise indicated that it sees you, do not continue to flash at it. Fire off a smoke device. If you have run out of flares, flash once in a while with the mirror to keep them on course.

MORSE CODE

A	•—	M	——	Y	—•——
B	—•••	N	—•	Z	——••
C	—•—•	O	———	1	•————
D	—••	P	•——•	2	••———
E	•	Q	——•—	3	•••——
F	••—•	R	•—•	4	••••—
G	——•	S	•••	5	•••••
H	••••	T	—	6	—••••
I	••	U	••—	7	——•••
J	•———	V	•••—	8	———••
K	—•—	W	•——	9	————•
L	•—••	X	—••—	0	—————

DISTRESS SIGNALS

International distress signals are designed to be displayed by vessels in trouble. Most are inappropriate for rafts. They include firing a gun at intervals of one minute; a fog horn sounding continuously; flames on a vessel; flying code flag November over code flag Charlie (NC, for "Yes/No," or "Not under Command"); or any square object over any round object; or waving your arms.

It seems to me that if rescuers can see your signal flags, they can see your big orange raft. And anyone seeing a raft with an orange canopy should guess that it's in trouble. However, Maurice and Maralyn Bailey found that a pair of oilskin pants tied to an upright oar in their dinghy was more visible than their raft, especially when the color wore off the raft canopy after a few weeks.

WATER

Death in a liferaft is usually due to exposure or thirst. A normal healthy, adult male needs about six pints of water a day. With proper care, you can last indefinitely on a pint a day, but no less. Your body needs that much to function. In the tropics, you may need two pints, about one liter, a day.

Castaways have gone for a week or more on one-third of a pint per day with no lasting consequences, but don't count on this. Castaways have also been found dead of dehydration with their water tanks half full. Don't ration less than a pint a day. The body requires that much to maintain itself.

If you have to ration water, as you probably will, divide it into several smaller portions over the day. Hold the water in your mouth as long as you can, then gargle before swallowing. This will rehydrate the tissues in your mouth and make you feel less thirsty.

The hazard of seasickness is not pain but dehydration. Vomiting makes the victim lose body fluids. Dispense pills to anyone susceptible to seasickness.

MINIMIZE URINATION

The easiest way to reduce the amount of water you need to take in is to reduce the amount you put out. Ordinarily, about half the water you consume goes back out as urine, one quarter as sweat, and one quarter as water vapor from the lungs.

The first day, drink no water at all. This will cause your body to activate some water-saving mechanisms, including reducing urination. You will need less water to survive. After the first day, you can start drinking your pint a day.

This does not apply to those who have survived drowning. They will have a raging thirst and need more water the first day, at least one full ration. If you have enough, give them more.

If you have a sure supply of water—regular rain or a hand-powered reverse-osmosis watermaker—this doesn't apply. Fill up all your jugs with water in case the rain stops or your watermaker breaks or falls overboard, and drink all you want. In most cases, however, you will have to be very careful about the water you take in and put out.

MINIMIZE SWEAT

Rest a lot. Do whatever work you have to do during the cooler parts of the day, at dawn and dusk. This will reduce both sweating and the amount of water expelled through the lungs.

Stay under the canopy. Only the watch should stick their heads out from under the canopy, and they should wear hats. Rotate the watch more frequently in the hot sun.

Throw sea water onto the canopy to cool it.

If there is no canopy, do whatever you can to make a sunshade: tie blankets to oars; hang shirts on strings; create as much shade as you can and put as much of yourselves in it as you can. If you have absolutely no way to make shade, take turns lying in each others' shadows. This is not for comfort; it is a matter of survival. Exposure and lack of water are what kill people in liferafts. This includes exposure to the sun.

DON'T DRINK SALT WATER

If you drink sea water, you will probably piss yourself to death. You'll die of dehydration sooner than if you hadn't drunk anything. The body needs to get rid of all the sodium in the salt so it increases urination, stealing fluids from other parts of the body. Once in a while you hear someone say that before you get dehydrated it's all right to supplement your fresh water ration with a small amount of sea water. This is not true. Never drink salt water.

DON'T DRINK URINE

Urine is full of substances your body is getting rid of. If you put it back in, the best you can hope for is that your body will get rid of it again, which will use up more fluid. I have heard people say it's all right to drink someone else's urine. This is not true; it's worse. Never drink urine.

DESALTING TABLETS

Each tablet will de-salt a pint of water. The water will look bad and taste bad, but you can drink it safely. Don't drink the sludge. Some rafts have a desalting kit with packets of chemical. These have a filter to get rid of the salt sludge. Follow the directions for the unit.

REVERSE-OSMOSIS WATERMAKERS

A hand-powered reverse-osmosis watermaker is the very best device you can have with you. Drop the hose with the filter into the sea or into a bucket of sea water. Pull on the handle. In about ten minutes, fresh water will start dripping from the other hose.

To get the maximum water flow, you'll have to pump 30-40 times a minute to keep an internal operating pressure of 800–1000 psi. It's something for the watch to do at night.

The manufacturer says that the seals and O-rings will need replacing after 600 to 700 hours. That's 25-28 days of continuous pumping. I hope you have spares.

A reverse-osmosis watermaker is the most important thing to have with you. If you have water, you can do nearly anything.

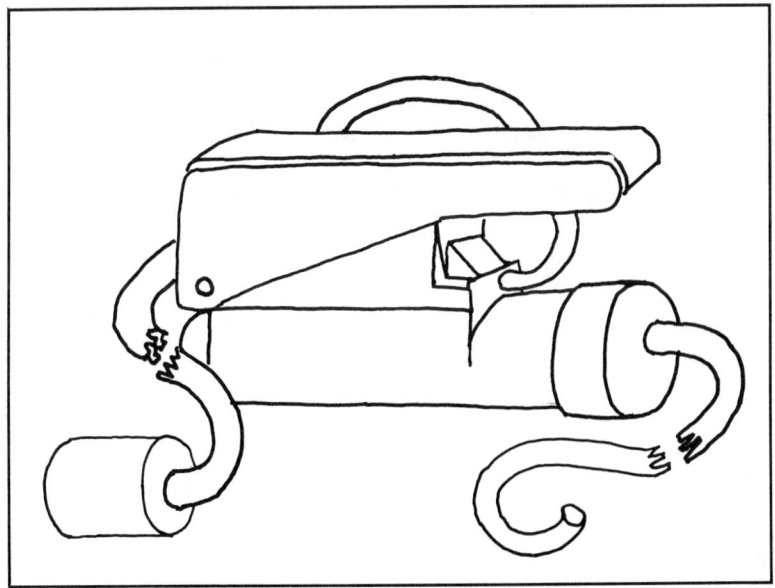

SOLAR STILLS

These come in various commercial styles, but essentially a solar still is just a balloon with a donut-shaped ballast ring at the throat. The center of the ballast ring is covered with fabric. When the fabric is wet, it's water-tight, and the balloon can be inflated. A black cloth wick is attached at several points inside the balloon.

You pour sea water into a cup on top of the balloon. The first half-gallon runs down a tube into the ballast ring. The rest of the sea water drips from the cup onto the wick. There is a jiggle string to keep the drip valve clear.

Water first saturates the wick and then evaporates. Vapor condenses on the inside of the balloon and runs down to the bottom and into a hose running to a collecting bottle. The bottle and hose trail in the water to keep cool.

There are three problems with solar stills: 1) They don't work when there's not enough sun; 2) They don't work in rough weather; and 3), they're fragile. Steve Callahan had two aboard, and neither one worked right. The balloons kept deflating, which caused the wicks to touch the balloon, which contaminated the fresh water.

You may have to operate the stills aboard the raft rather than floating them in the sea. If so, make sure the fabric across the bottom stays wet, to keep air in.

MAKING A SOLAR STILL

If you have a bucket and some plastic, you can make a solar still. Place a cup in the center of the bottom of the bucket. This is to catch the fresh water. Saturate some cloth or other absorbent material with sea water and wrap it around the cup. This is to keep the sea water from sloshing around. Stretch a piece of plastic over the bucket, with a weight in the center to form a cone pointing downward at the cup in the bucket. Tie the plastic around the outside of the bucket so it touches the rim all around. To improve efficiency and speed of condensation, you can put cold sea-water into the plastic on top.

If you have some flexible plastic tubing, tie one end inside the water cup and the other end outside the bucket, so you don't have to take the still apart to get water out. Otherwise, it will take up to an hour or so for the air to resaturate after you take a drink.

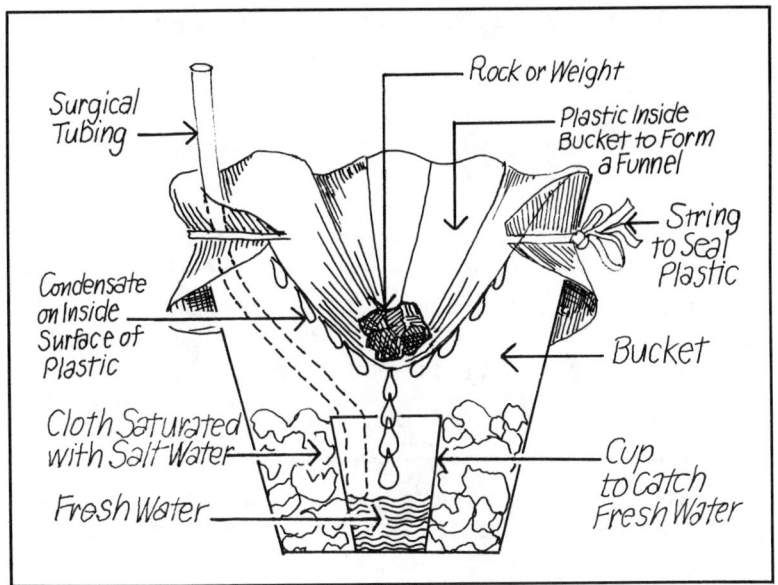

A solar still can be made from a bucket, a cup, and a plastic bag.

RAINWATER

If you do not have a reverse-osmosis watermaker or satisfactory solar stills, you may need to sail toward a place where you can find rain to maintain your water supply. See the chapter on navigation for information on how to find one of these places and the chapter on the raft for how to rig a sail for propulsion.

How to Catch Rain

An inflatable raft has a catchment system which consists of a pair of rain gutters which direct the run-off into a tube which goes inside the raft. The system does collect rain, but the water is often unpalatable because the first water from any rain is contaminated by salt which has dried onto the canopy since the last rain. And after a week or two, any rain will be full of flakes of yellow or orange paint from the raft.

The easiest way to get clean rainwater is to stretch a piece of clean plastic such as a space blanket across the part of the canopy that catches the rain. This will keep the salt and paint from ending up in the fresh water.

Tie a piece of plastic to two paddles and hold it out of a door to direct rain inside to your water jugs.

If you have both rainwater and packaged water, use the rainwater first.

SEA ICE

You can harvest sea ice and melt it for drinking water. Sea ice formed last year is salt-free. This year's ice is still salty. New ice is opaque and angular. Old ice is clear and smooth and it splinters easily.

ENEMAS

If you have some water that is not salty or poisonous but is too disgusting to drink, you can absorb as much as a pint a day—enough to keep alive on—through the large intestine. The problem is getting it in there. A solar shower will work, but the nozzle may be painfully large and have to be cut off. Dougal Robertson recommends a tube taken from the boarding ladder on his raft.

Lay the victim face-down with one knee drawn up. Lubricate the tube with vaseline, fish grease, sweat, or spit. Stick it in the rectum about 3 inches and let the water flow in by gravity.

Be gentle. Tomorrow may be your turn in the barrel.

FOOD

Food is not as big a problem as water. It is not as hard to get; you need less than you probably think; and you can last longer without any. A normal man should survive 30 or 40 days with no food at all. Many of us have enough fat to extend that time.

Most liferafts and lifeboats provide only some hard candy or vitamin-enriched bread as food. The candy has more psychological than nutritional value and the bread is skimpy. If you have freeze-dried or other dehydrated food with you, eat it only when you have enough water to wash it down and to digest it. Otherwise, you will just plug yourselves up.

You will have to seek other sources of nourishment. Start fishing right away, so you can make the packaged food last as long as possible. Save it for times when you cannot fish: during bad weather, when the fish are not biting, you lose the gear overboard, or what you have already caught goes bad.

VITAMINS

If you have vitamin pills, take them regularly. Fish do not provide vitamins. Without them you will be subject to scurvy and anemia. In a few weeks your mouth may begin to hurt.

SEAWEEDS

Seaweed is a good source of vitamins. Nearly all seaweeds are edible, but they have few usable calories. They are about half cellulose, which humans cannot digest. A few threadlike or slender branching seaweeds have acids in them which can irritate the stomach, but garden-variety broad-leafed seaweed that you find floating in the ocean does not.

Seaweeds do have vitamins, minerals and fiber, which makes them nutritious if not nourishing. And they have protein, as much as 10 per cent to 20 per cent of the dry weight.

Rinse it first. Seaweeds are also covered with salt. If you do not have enough water to rinse it and to drink with it, you had better not eat any. You can pick up some seaweed when you happen across it and wait until it rains before eating it. It dries easily in the meantime.

Even if you are not interested in eating the seaweed, investigate every patch you encounter. You will often find small fish or crabs mixed in. Crabs found on reefs are sometimes poisonous, but seaweed crabs should be all right. Eat the whole thing, but chew it up well.

One poisonous creature looks like seaweed but is not. It is called stinging seaweed, but it is actually a hydroid, related to the sea anemone. It grows only a few inches high. It's found on the bottom, usually on coral reefs, in tropical waters. Seaweeds you find floating in mid–ocean are very unlikely to be this.

PLANKTON

Individual plankton are tiny creatures that drift instead of swim. Collectively plankton looks like gray scum and tastes like sawdust and paste, but it's very good for you. Mix it with turtle eggs, if you have them, to make it palatable.

The only way to get plankton is to tow a plankton net. But you must be moving faster than the current to catch any. Ideal speed is two knots relative to the water. You can trip the sea anchor to go faster. (You might even pull in the sea anchor from time to time to see if it has captured any.)

Fast or slow, towing a net is worth a try, since plankton is so nutritious. Tow it right at the surface. Plankton concentrate there because that's where the light for photosynthesis is. Ninety percent of the earth's photosynthesis goes on near the surface of the oceans.

BARNACLES

Barnacles start out as free-floating organisms. They attach to something and grow up there. Everything that floats and every rock at the edge of the sea seems to have them, even slow-swimming whales. There are more individual barnacles in the world than there are mosquitoes.

Horseneck barnacles are usually the first to appear on the bottom of a raft. They grow on a short stalk. If you're in the raft for a few weeks, they should get big enough to eat.

They are difficult to get at attached to the bottom of the raft. You would have to jump in the water to harvest them. If you trail a bit of heaving line in order to observe your course, barnacles will attach to it. If you float sheet plastic in the water around your raft (to reduce sharks' rubbing; see page 85), barnacles will attach to the plastic and be easy to harvest.

Eat the whole thing. The shell is calcium carbonate, which is good for you.

BIRDS

The easiest way to catch a bird is with a hook and line. Float bait on the water without a sinker and let the bird eat it. Let it take the bait long enough to get the hook in its mouth.

The best bait is fish guts or meat. If you don't have any, you might try a bit of fish skin or cloth tied a few inches above the hook. When the bird sets down to examine it, jerk the line and snag the bird with the trailing hook. It works better with a treble hook. The crew of *H.M.S. Bounty* had good luck doing this.

If you don't have bait or hooks, try a snare. Float a loop of monofilament in the water with a piece of cloth or something in the center of it, and hope the bird puts its neck in the snare to examine the cloth. This is much less likely to succeed, but you can only do what you have the tools for.

Many sea birds will land on a raft, or even on your shoulder. Be quick and grab them. When you have a bird in hand, kill it by pulling and twisting its neck in a single vigorous motion.

Skin it, eat everything but the intestines, and then scrape and suck the inside of the skin. On land, when you have a fire to cook the bird, it is best to pluck it rather than skin it, because much of the fat is attached to the skin. But skinning is much easier than plucking, especially if you don't have boiling water to scald it.

Depending on how much other food you have, you can chew up and eat the bones. Some have marrow inside.

Reactions to eating raw sea bird vary. The Baileys ate boobies and noddies whenever they could catch them and described the meat as sweet. They also got fresh flying fish from the gullets of the boobies. Others say the best you can hope for in a sea bird is that it will be salty, stringy, and unpleasant. Some people are unable to keep raw bird down. If you cannot, you can still get some moisture out of it by sucking on pieces of it.

If your fishing lures are not working well, or if they've been badly chewed up, you can use the bird's feathers or carcass to spruce them up or to make new lures. Save some of the feathers just in case.

TURTLES

Except in a few places, the turtles you find in the open ocean are good to eat. (See page 48 for information on turtle poisoning. If any part is poisonous, it is most likely the liver.)

Ocean-going turtles are in danger of extinction. If the idea of killing one and eating it strikes you as morally offensive, you're not hungry enough to do it. But at some point you may become more endangered than they are. Some castaways have lived more or less entirely on turtles.

The best way to catch a turtle is to grab it or gaff it by the hind flippers. Turn it onto its back and pull it into the raft. Count on getting scratched when you do this.

Be careful if there are barnacles on the turtle's shell; they can tear the raft.

Watch out for the beak. It bites.

The best way to kill a turtle is to slit its throat. It will go faster if you cut the arteries on both sides.

Be ready to catch the blood. It's liquid, it's nutritious, and it's tasty even when you aren't hungry. If you don't have any empty containers, make a sheet of plastic into a bag, or drink it straight from the turtle.

The best way to open up a turtle is to slice between the top and bottom shells. Start at the neck and cut inboard of the legs. When you have cut all the way around, you will have to reach in at the head end and cut some ligaments holding the bottom shell on.

All the meat is concentrated around the legs. Hack out as much as you can and put it in a container for an hour or so to collect the fluid that oozes from it. Mix this fluid with turtle eggs or with dried meat or fish.

If the weather is humid, the meat may turn bad, so eat as much as you can while it's fresh. Chew on the bones. Those inside the flippers are easiest to get at. The leg bones have a tasty marrow in them. Chew off the end and use something long and pointed to scrape the marrow out, or twist the ends in opposite directions to make a spiral fracture. Dry what you cannot eat. Cut it into thin strips and hang them on a line stretched across the raft.

Throw the shell overboard when you are rescued. If you take it ashore, someone with no compassion is liable to arrest you for killing a member of an endangered species.

FISH

Fish are your most likely source of food on a liferaft. How to catch and clean them is discussed later in this chapter, starting on page 49.

Once you have caught a fish, you can eat everything but the innards, and you can even eat some of that. As usual, it depends on how hungry you are. On Day Two, you might want to skip eating the eyes, brain, and heart, but on Day 75 you will probably look forward to them. Never eat the liver, intestines, or roe of a tropical fish.

Stomach contents may or may not be edible, depending on how far gone they are and how hungry you are. In any case, you will have to wash them to get rid of stomach acids before trying them. Taste it carefully.

The area around the eye has a lot of moisture you can suck out. The eye itself has a squirt of moisture in it. Bite it.

The cheeks have a small amount of particularly tasty meat. So does the area just above the eyes.

Scrape and suck the inside of the skin. It may have some fat on it.

The backbone of a bony fish has fluid in it that can be sucked out. Sharks do not have this fluid.

Bones can be eaten. Just chew them or chop them well before swallowing. If you are short on water the bones might not be fully broken down when they have to pass through your various sphincters.

If anything is left, dry it to eat later. (See page 59 for a discussion of drying fish.)

CAUTION — Poisonous Fish

Some fish are poisonous to eat. Also, many fish in tropical waters (in particular the tropical Pacific, Caribbean, and Indian Oceans), are poisonous because of their diet. (See page 44 for a more complete list and a discussion of the poison.)

Most fish fluids are all right to drink, but a few are not. Taste a little. If it is bitter or salty, do not drink it. Taste any unknown food with caution.

CAUTION — Eating Fish without Water

Some authorities say you should not eat protein on days when you have less than two pints of water to drink. Your body needs that much water to make the gastric juices for digestion. This is more true for dried fish than for fresh, which has a lot of moisture in it. Castaways have eaten fish whenever they could and survived just fine.

It is true that if you do not have enough water to wash it through, whatever you eat stays in you, but castaways have gone 30 days in a raft without a bowel movement and come through all right. (The first one was a doozy, though, and left them weak and dizzy.) If you eat some seaweed with the fish, the bulk will be increased, but so will the salt.

One way to deal with this problem is to eat fresh fish (or glucose or carbohydrates) when you have less water and eat dried fish when you have more water. Naturally this presumes you have a choice.

If you don't have a choice of fresh, dried, or packaged, remember that you have to eat enough to stay coherent and strong enough to catch more fish.

If you have less than one pint of water per day, do not eat fish. You can get by without food for a few days, and you run the risk of dehydration if you make your body use all its water for digestion.

LIKELY VICTIMS

Dorado

Dorado is also known as mahi-mahi or dolphin fish. Dorado is the Spanish name and mahi-mahi is Hawaiian. I call them dorado because I live and fish closer to Mexico than to Hawaii and because if you call them dolphin fish, someone invariably thinks you're talking about porpoises. They are not— repeat, not—Flipper. Flipper has lungs and red meat. Dorado are ordinary fish with gills and fish meat. They just happen to have the same name.

Dorado are easy to catch because they will take any kind of bait or lure. They are easy to spear because they will swim slowly by the raft. They will take up the raft as a home base and keep coming back for you to pick them off one at a time.

Dorado are excellent eating cooked and are as good raw as any fish can be. How good that is depends on how much you like sushi. If you are reading this in a liferaft, you probably like it well enough. Dorado meat dries better than many other kinds.

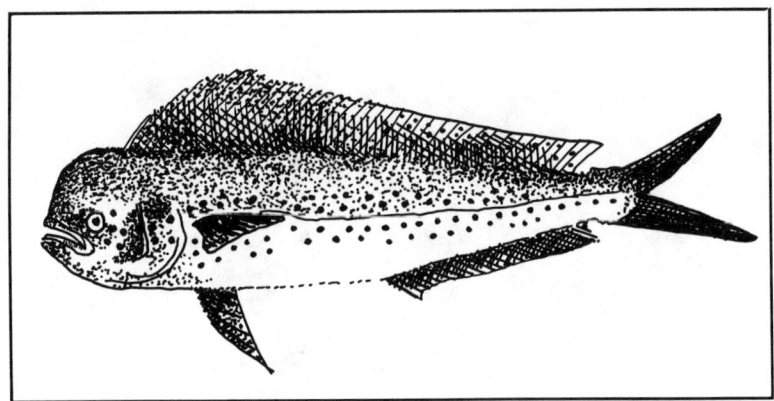

Dorado (good to eat).

The only problem with dorado is that they thrash wildly when they come out of the water. A big one can beat you severely. A small one can slash you or the raft with the hook in its mouth. Any size can jump back into the water.

The skin of dorado is very tough. Before plastic, commercial fishermen used it to keep tuna from chewing the feathers off their lures. You might find a use for it on a raft, but when it gets wet, it becomes extremely slippery.

Most schools of dorado in the open ocean are made up of females. Females have a low, sloping forehead. Males have a bulging, squared-off forehead. They can be silver, yellow, blue, or green. I have heard of red ones but never seen any. They have irregular fluorescent blue spots all over their sides in life. Sometimes (as in the Red Sea), they have vertical bands of dark green. The shape is always the same, long, deep, and skinny. When they are hungry or excited, they light up, and their lips and pectoral fins become fluorescent, too. In the bottom of the boat they turn all these colors in rapid sequence and then die dull gray.

Triggerfish

Triggerfish will readily eat small chunks of anything, including each other. Try a wire leader on your smallest hook first. If they do not bite that, try it without the wire. They can also be speared.

To get a triggerfish to put down its trigger (the front spine on its dorsal fin), press on its forehead just in front of the spine and push the spine back.

Triggerfish have an extremely tough hide. They are nearly impossible to get into without a good knife.

Sometimes triggerfish are poisonous. As is explained in the section on ciguatera poisoning, page 45, this is caused by eating corals and other

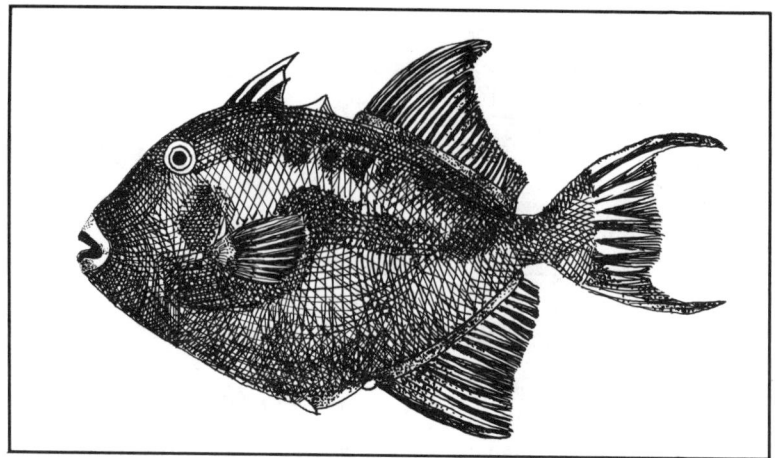

Triggerfish (good to eat).

poisonous creatures. Open ocean triggerfish should be all right, and some castaways have lived almost entirely on them. Still, if you have a choice, eat a different kind of fish. If you don't have a choice, eat what you have, but soak the fillets in water for half an hour before you eat them.

Tuna

There are many kinds of tuna in the ocean. They range in size from half a pound to over half a ton. All have pointed noses and bullet shapes. A few have white meat, but most have red meat. This red meat is a heat exchanger. Tunas are warmer than the surrounding water. Their constant swimming burns up calories.

Tuna seldom eat chunks of bait on a hook. They do take lures. You will seldom see them close enough to the raft to use cast-and-retrieve lures. You'll be more likely to catch them trolling. They like their lures retrieved very fast. Big ones will take your gear away from you.

Most tuna are easy to deal with after you catch them. Some quiver and beat their tails, but they are not as flexible as dorado, so they cannot jump around inside the raft. They will stop beating their tails if you cover their eyes. Small ones can be gripped behind the head.

Yellowfin tuna is called *ahi* in Japanese and is one of the most esteemed fish for sashimi. The belly meat is most prized, because it has the most fat.

Do not try to dry leftover tuna. Gorge yourself and throw away anything that is left after a few hours. The flesh is softer than dorado or triggerfish and goes bad quickly. Bad tuna gives you scombroid poisoning, which is a particularly unpleasant condition, though seldom fatal. (See page 46.) Of course, they go bad quicker in hot weather than in cold.

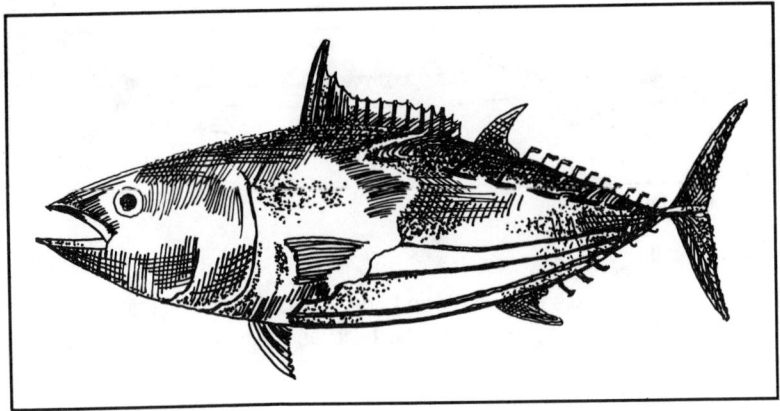

Skipjack tuna (good to eat).

Wahoo

Wahoo are very strong and have the sharpest teeth I have ever seen. They bite lures readily, but they often bite them in half. The teeth aren't pointed; they're round, like a serrated knife. They cut through the heaviest line as though it were not there. If they catch it right, they can cut through heavy wire. Accidentally brushing up against a dead one can gash a leg. The only way you'll ever catch one is if a small one bites a lure on your heaviest wire at the end of your heaviest line.

They also jump, and people have been disembowelled by them. Several times I have seen them jump right into the boat when someone was retrieving a lure. If you are using cast-and-retrieve lures and wahoo are around, let the lure stop dead before you lift it out of the water, or you may find a wahoo in the raft with you. This would not be a pleasant experience. Its teeth are sharp enough to go straight through the bottom of your raft.

The other unpleasant thing about wahoo is their slime. It is extreme. The only good thing about it is that it will wash off after it dries.

That said, wahoo is one of the best eating fish in the ocean. They are mostly found near islands or ocean ridges in tropical waters. Don't worry about the ugly creature in its stomach. It's a parasite. They all have them.

Wahoo (good to eat).

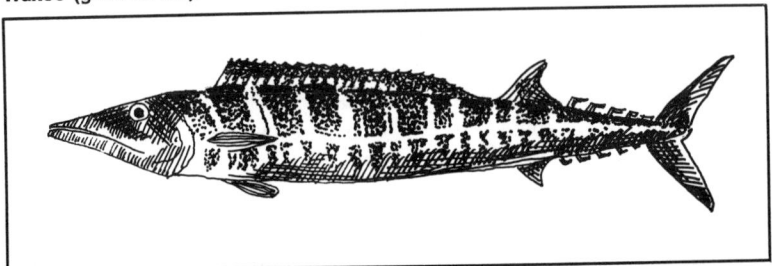

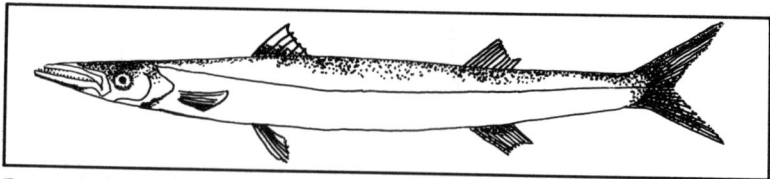

Barracuda (good to eat).

Flying Fish

You can't catch these on a hook and line, but they will sometimes fly into the raft. After you eat the body, the head and pectoral fins make pretty good bait.

Pilot Fish

These are lovely fish with black and dark blue vertical bands. They follow sharks and eat whatever tidbits fall off the sharks' prey. They will bite live bait. I've never tried to catch them with a lure.

Remora

These follow sharks, too. They hold onto the shark with a suction-like gripper on the top of their head. Like pilot fish, remoras eat what falls out of a shark's mouth. They take bait on a hook just fine. I've never eaten one, but I did fillet one once, in the Red Sea. The meat was white and firm, but I've heard others describe it as gray and mushy. This may vary from ocean to ocean or may depend on what they eat. The Baileys ate one after about a hundred days in a raft in the Pacific and said they liked it.

Barracuda

These have nasty teeth, too, though not nearly as bad as the wahoo. They will sometimes take chunk bait, but you will probably have better luck with lures, especially feathered ones. Use heavy wire because they can bite a lure in half. Be careful when you bring the fish in. Try to land it with its mouth on your survival bag or something similar to protect the raft from its teeth.

Barracuda are not quite as slimy as wahoo, but stickier. You can't wash the slime off. If it dries on you, it will still be slimy when you get it wet again.

Barracuda are found mostly near shore or over ocean ridges, although I have seen them a hundred miles offshore around oil-field platforms above an otherwise featureless bottom.

Barracuda are sometimes poisonous—especially in the Caribbean— depending on what they've been eating. (See page 45.)

Mola Mola (Ocean Sunfish)

Mola Mola is Latin for millstone millstone. And the mola mola is built like a millstone with fins. It is the biggest nonshark fish in the ocean. The record measured 10 feet long, 14 feet high at the fins, and weighed 4,928 pounds.

The mola mola is a very primitive fish. The body is rigid. The only place it bends is where the fins join the body. It has no air bladder and sinks rapidly when it dies. It has no lateral line, so it has no sense of touch. They bump into things and don't notice. They have no scales. Their skin is covered with denticles, like sharks. Under this is a soft pad of sticky gunk, which may be as thick as three inches on a big one. Most of the rest is guts and goo.

They swim just off vertical, flapping their fins like birds, and can get up enough speed to jump several feet out of the water.

Only about 20 per cent of the body weight is meat. The only muscles that do anything are in the throat, to pump water through the gills, and those that move the fins. The folks at the California Sea Grant Marine Advisory Program tell me the meat is edible. They say it is "jellylike, more like lobster or turtle than finfish." I've never met anyone hungry enough to try it.

Mola Mola (ocean sunfish) (barely edible).

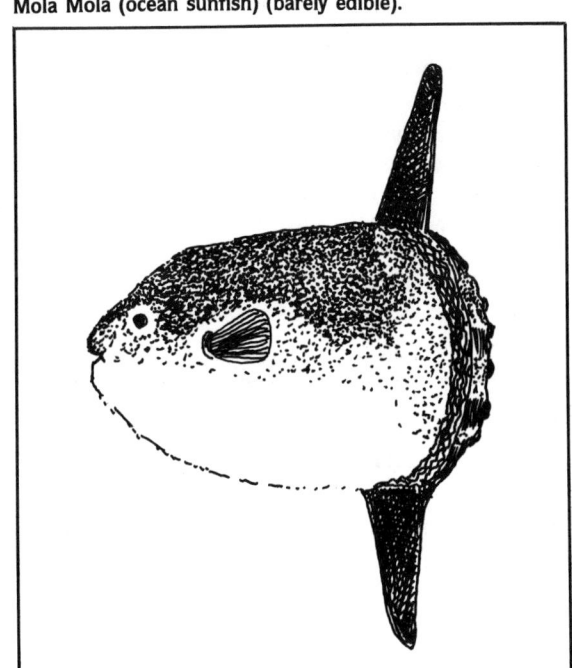

Sharks

Catching a shark in a liferaft is a bad idea except as a last resort. If a shark eats bait intended for another fish, your best bet is to try to break the line as near the hook as possible. Give the line a sharp jerk.

Sharks have sharp teeth and are immediate and tenacious in their use. Mostly they will take your bait, hook, and leader away with them. If you're "lucky" enough to catch one, it may stay alive enough to bite you for a very long time. It also stands a good chance of chewing through the raft.

If, after all this, you insist on trying to catch a shark, use your biggest hook and your heaviest wire and swivel. If the shark is more than half as big as you are, do not tie anything strong (wire, heaving line) to the raft or to yourself.

When you get the shark up to the raft, kill it before you bring it in. The simplest way to do this is to stick an oar in its mouth to keep it occupied and stab it in the eye with your longest knife.

When you get it to the raft, drag it in tail first and cut off the head while it's still hanging out over the water, so any random thrashes won't sink you.

None of this is easy or safe.

If you manage to catch a small shark, your safest grip is behind the head. Next best is by the tail, but the shark can still twist around and bite you. Cut off the head immediately.

Clean any dead shark right away. Sharks pass wastes through the skin, and some taste like urea if you do not clean and skin them immediately. Others taste like urea no matter what you do.

Do not eat the liver. Many sharks have poisonous livers. Only a few sharks have poisonous meat, and they're all too big to catch. Eating the liver can be fatal.

CREATURES DANGEROUS TO EAT

Poisonous Fish

Few fish are poisonous by themselves, but many become poisonous due to what they eat, usually algae, dinoflagellates, or poisonous invertebrates. Sometimes fish in a particular place can be good to eat and then suddenly become poisonous and stay that way for years.

Ciguatera Poisoning

This kind of poisoning is most common near islands in the tropical Caribbean and the Pacific and Indian Oceans, because that is where the poisonous fish-food is found.

The first symptom is often a sharp metallic taste in the mouth, which can occur as soon as you eat it. Other symptoms include tingling of the lips, tongue, and limbs; upset stomach; aching joints; severe weakness; and feeling hot things as cold and cold things as an electric shock. Bad cases can involve neurological problems, including loss of coordination and reflexes, tremors, convulsions, coma, or paralysis.

About twelve per cent of cases are said to result in death, sometimes in as little as 15 minutes. If you live through it, it may take months or even years to fully recover. It is not something to fool around with.

Prevention: The best way to prevent ciguatera poisoning is not to eat poisonous fish. Unfortunately, you cannot tell one by looking at it, although fish which are unusually big around in proportion to their length should be treated with caution.

Avoid barracuda and jacks during their reproductive seasons. You can tell it is this time when female fish are carrying eggs and males have testes, which are long, milky—white organs.

Never eat the roe of tropical fish. Ciguatera poisoning depends not on the species but on what the individual fish has been eating, and it often concentrates in the roe, so you should throw away the roe of any fish you eat. It is true that many people have eaten roe with no problems, but it is nonetheless not worth the risk unless you know the species and the area. This does not apply to turtle eggs, which are not poisonous.

Since coral-eaters are subject to ciguatera poisoning, do not eat fish that eat coral. These are generally recognizable by their protruding front teeth.

Another way to avoid ciguatera is to cut the fish into thin strips and soak them for at least half an hour in several changes of water. The poison is moderately water soluble. If you use fresh water for the soak, throw the water away afterwards.

A word of caution: heat does not affect this poison. If you cook the fish it will not weaken the poison at all. Boiling may leach out some of the poison, but be sure to throw away the water.

Once again: never eat the liver, intestines, or roe of any tropical fish.

Treatment: The only treatment for ciguatera poisoning is to induce vomiting before too much of it gets into the system. If you have a cathartic, use it. If not, try warm salt water or a finger down the throat.

According to *Dangerous Marine Animals*, by Bruce Halstead, the following fish have been known to cause ciguatera poisoning in the following places. Many of these are important food fish at other times or in other places.

Anchovy: Off China, Japan, Korea or Formosa.

Barracuda: Indian, Pacific, and West Atlantic Oceans, Caribbean Sea

Chinaman Fish: Australia

Filefish: All warm seas.

Herring: Tropical Pacific, Asia, India

Jack Crevalle: Tropical Atlantic

Blue Star Jack: All warm seas and Japan

Ladyfish: All warm seas.

Moray Eel: Pacific and Indian Oceans from Hawaii westward to East Africa and from Japan to Australia

Oceanic Bonito: All tropical seas

Parrotfish: Caribbean Sea, Indian and Pacific Oceans

Porgie: Eastern Atlantic, Mediterranean and Black Seas

Grouper and seabass: Various kinds are implicated in tropical seas all over the world

Red Snapper: Tropical Indian and Pacific Oceans, Red Sea

Squaretail: Temperate waters all over the world

Squirrelfish: Indian and Pacific Oceans

Surgeonfish: Hawaii and Johnston Islands

Goatfish: Polynesia, westward to East Africa

Triggerfish: Tropical Pacific, from Polynesia westward to Africa and north to China and Japan

Trunkfish: Tropical Pacific and the tropical Atlantic, north to Cape Cod

Wrasse: Tropical Indian and Pacific Oceans

Scombroid Poisoning

This comes from tuna left out of the water too long. Any member of the tuna family can cause it, including bonito, skipjack, and mackerel, which are the likeliest ones for you to catch. It can develop in a fish in a couple of hours. Paleness in the gills or a bad smell are signs. Remember, after some time on a raft, your sense of smell is probably blunted.

Symptoms usually come on quickly. Often you can tell right away that the fish is bad because of a peppery taste. Symptoms include headache, dizziness, flushing, itching, rash, stomachache, burning throat, heart palpitations, nausea, vomiting, diarrhea, thirst, inability to swallow, and suffocation. It is seldom fatal. Victims usually recover in a day or two.

The best medicine for scombroid poisoning is to avoid it. If it occurs, however, treat the victim for shock, and administer antihistamines if you you have them.

Shark Poisoning

This usually comes from eating shark livers, but a few large tropical sharks and the Greenland shark have caused poisoning in people who ate their flesh.

Symptoms start in half an hour with nausea, vomiting, diarrhea, stomachache, headache, joint aches, tingling around the mouth, and a burning sensation in the mouth, throat, and esophagus. They can progress to lack of coordination, difficulty in breathing due to paralysis, coma, and death.

Hallucinogenic Fish Poisoning

Eating a few varieties of tropical reef fish, such as goat fish, sometimes causes hallucinations. They come on within a couple of hours and last a day or more. Other symptoms include dizziness, lack of coordination, stomachache, nausea, vomiting, and mental depression. Frequently the chest feels tightly constricted.

This is all very scary to the victim, but no one is known to have died from it. As fish poisonings go, it is fairly mild.

Puffer Poisoning

This is not mild at all. Puffers are among the most poisonous of all sea creatures. They also bite and smell bad. They can be recognized by the way they puff themselves up with water or air when frightened. Avoid any fish that does this. The group includes puffers, globefish, blowfish, toadfish, porcupinefishes, and ocean sunfishes (not the same as Mola Mola).

The flesh of puffers is generally safe and tasty. The poison is in the liver, gonads, intestines, and skin. The problem is getting to the meat

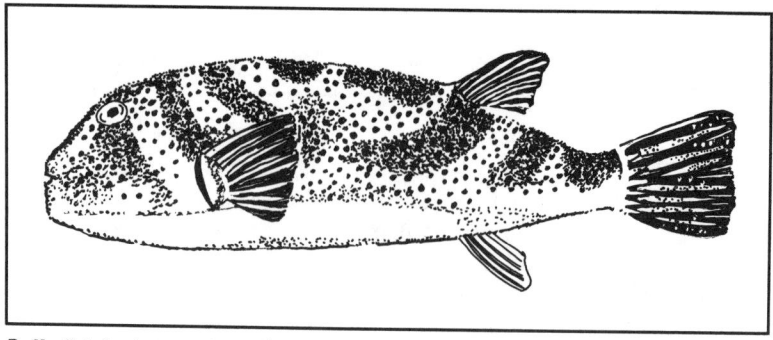

Pufferfish (poisonous to eat).

without touching anything else. In Japan chefs must be specially trained and licensed to prepare it. And they still lose people. It is not worth the risk.

Symptoms include a tingling of the lips and skin which spreads over the whole body; there may be stomachache; breathing becomes difficult. This can progress to uncoordination, tremors, convulsions, and paralysis. The fatality rate is about 60 per cent. There is no treatment.

Turtle Poisoning

As with fish, turtles are usually safe but sometimes eat things that make them poisonous to people. This seems to be most common around the Philippines, Sri Lanka, and Indonesia. As usual, whether you want to take the chance depends on how hungry you are.

The liver is especially dangerous and should never be eaten.

Symptoms usually develop within a few hours but may not show up for several days. They start with nausea, vomiting, diarrhea, severe stomachache, dizziness, and a burning sensation in the mouth and throat. Swallowing becomes difficult and saliva profuse. This may take a while to develop, but it gets worse. The breath becomes foul. The tongue developes a white coating, often accompanied by small, red papules, which may open up into ulcers. The last symptom before death is usually extreme sleepiness.

About 45 per cent of the victims die. There is no treatment.

Paralytic Shellfish Poisoning

This usually comes from eating mussels, cockles, or clams that have eaten poisonous dinoflagellates. These are the critters that make up a red tide, but they can make sea animals poisonous even if there are not enough of them around to make a red tide. They are found mostly in the temperate latitudes during the warm season, between March and November in the northern hemisphere, and September and May in the southern hemisphere. Symptoms start with tingling or burning in the lips, mouth, and face. This spreads over the body. The tingling becomes numbness, and the numbness may become paralysis. Victims usually feel weak, dizzy, and extremely thirsty. Their joints ache. They salivate excessively but have difficulty swallowing. Symptoms seldom include nausea, vomiting, diarrhea, or stomachache.

There is no treatment beyond vomiting up the poison immediately after eating it.

This is of most importance to you if you wash up on shore. I've never heard of it happening to barnacles on a raft, but if you find yourself in a red tide, do not eat barnacles. You can recognize a red tide in the daytime by its dull red color. At night, the sea is exceptionally bioluminescent.

Tropical Reef Crab Poisoning

If you wash ashore on a tropical reef, do not eat crabs unless you see someone else eat them safely first. The poison is similar to that in puffers, but perhaps not quite so severe. Death is less common.

FISHING TECHNIQUES

Monofilament Line

Nylon monofilament line (mono) is so slick that it requires special knots. Many knots which work on braided lines will not hold in mono.

In tying any knot with monofilament line, wet the line before you cinch it tight. Friction from tightening the knot creates heat which weakens the line as much as 15 per cent. But if the line is wet, the heat is dissipated without damaging the line. Spit works fine. So does salt water.

Hold the hook with a pair of pliers when you pull the knot tight, or hook it over a loop of string.

Monofilament line is very fine and a small reduction in diameter can cause the loss of a fish. Every time you catch a fish, examine the line near the knot. It may be frayed. If you see the slightest nick, or if it looks or feels stretched, cut the line and retie the knot.

Knots

<u>Palomar Knot</u> This is the best knot to tie hooks on with your 20# and 40# line. It is the strongest of the easy-to-tie knots, with nearly 100 per cent strength. Of the strong ones, it is the easiest to tie. It is harder to tie with heavy line or to use with lures.

To tie a palomar knot, first double the line back on itself for several inches. Then stick the doubled part through the eye of the hook.

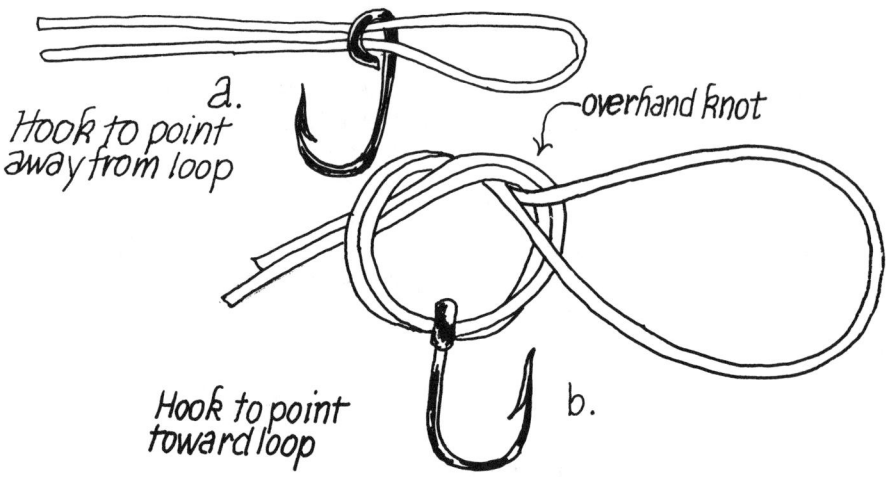

Tie a simple overhand knot in the doubled part of the line.

Put the hook through the end loop.

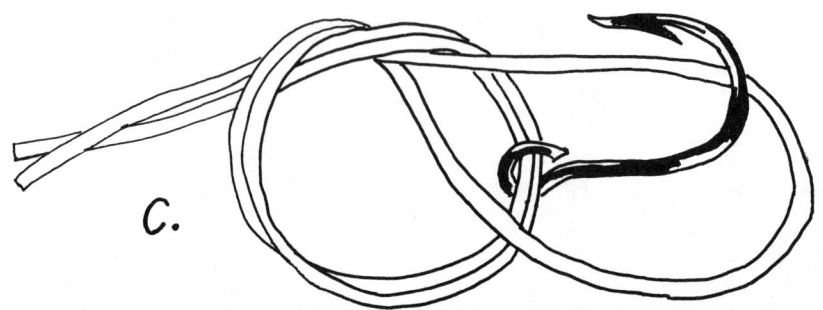

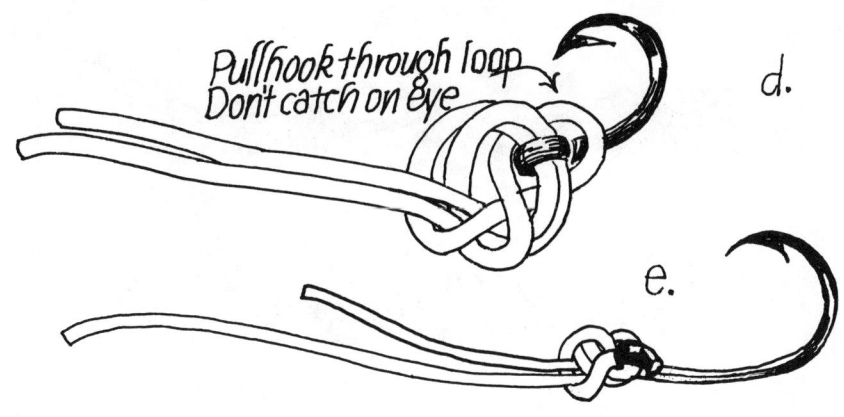

Wet the knot, hold the hook in a pair of pliers (or hook it over something), and pull the knot tight. Cut off the excess monofilament.

Be careful that the line does not hang up at the joint

Improved Clinch Knot This is for tying on lures and for tying hooks onto heavy line.

First stick the line through the eye of the hook.

Then either spin the hook or wrap the line around five or six times.

Then put the end of the line through the gap between the eye of the hook and the first twist of the line. Then put the end of the line back through the loop you just made. Skip this step with your heaviest line (100#).

Wet the knot and pull it tight. Cut off the excess line.

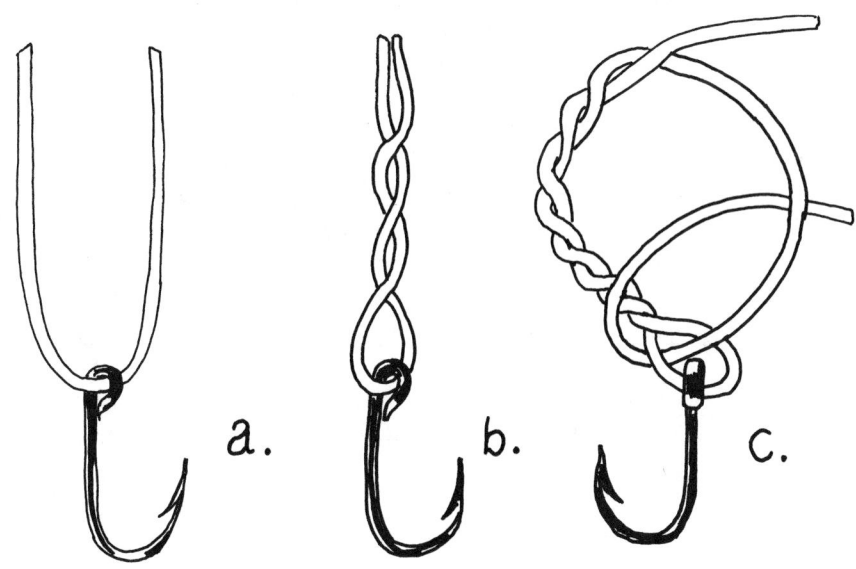

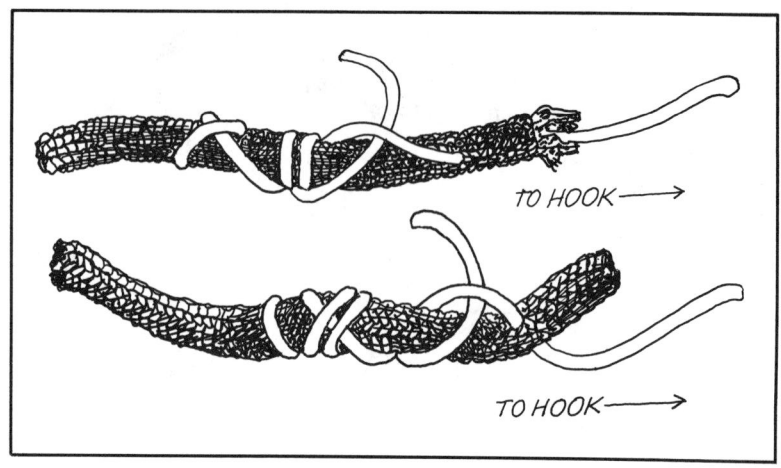

TO HOOK →

TO HOOK →

Tying Monofilament to a Heaving Line

The best way to secure monofilament to a heaving line is with a swivel. If you don't have one, the next best solution depends on the condition of your heaving line. If the end is securely closed (such as melted solid at the tip), you can thread the monofilament sideways through the heaving line and tie a clinch knot in it.

If the heaving line end is taped or frayed, stick the mono straight into the heaving line and then through the side of it and then tie a clinch knot.

Before You Start Fishing

Put something down on the raft floor to flop the fish onto. This will protect the raft and your hands from hooks, spears, and gaffs in case the fish thrashes around. The best thing would be a spare blanket folded on top of the fish-cleaning board. You can jam the spear-point or gaff-hook into the blanket.

This is especially important when you are fishing for dorado. Minimize the number of holes the fish can jump through. If the raft has two entrances, close the one you're not fishing from unless you need the ventilation.

Fishing with a Gaff

This is the quickest way to get a fish into the raft. All you have to do is put the gaff in the water and wait until a fish swims near enough. Many kinds of fish seem to like living under floating things, such as kelp patties and drifting rafts, either for the safety of the shadow or for the food they find there. Triggerfish and dorado eat the barnacles that live on the raft's bottom.

The problem with gaff-fishing is that it's tiring and boring because you have to stand ready until a fish swims by. And, if you're using a home-made gaff, it's likely to break frequently.

To make a gaff, secure your biggest hook to a dowel or oar handle. Use a hose clamp if you have it. If you don't, you'll have to use string to make the gaff strong and rigid. In this case, tie the hook onto the shaft three ways:

1. Tie a line through the eye and around the shaft. The hook should dangle just past the end of the shaft, pointed outward.
2. Strap down the shaft of the hook with string, wire or tape. Even if you pull the gaff straight, there will always be sideways pressure on the hook when the fish flops, so this line will break frequently.
3. Tie a line from the eye of the hook back to the raft, so as not to lose the fish or the hook if it comes loose from the handle. The best method for this is to run a wire from the hook to a heaving line. Tie the heaving line to the raft. Make it short, so the fish can't get a running start. If you use monofilament, have someone else hold this line to play the fish if it breaks the hook loose from the gaff. Do not tie the monofilament to anything, because sudden stress can snap it.

To fish with the gaff, put it in the water hook-upward and wait for a fish to swim by. The best place to stick a fish is in the belly just behind the head. This will point it toward the raft and it is less likely to develop enough power swimming to tear out the hook. By sticking it in the belly you turn the fish upside-down, which makes it harder for it to swim. Also, if you are a little slow reacting, the gaff will go into the belly near the anus rather than into the back behind the dorsal. The tissue near the anus is the strongest and the hook is unlikely to tear out.

A home-made gaff.

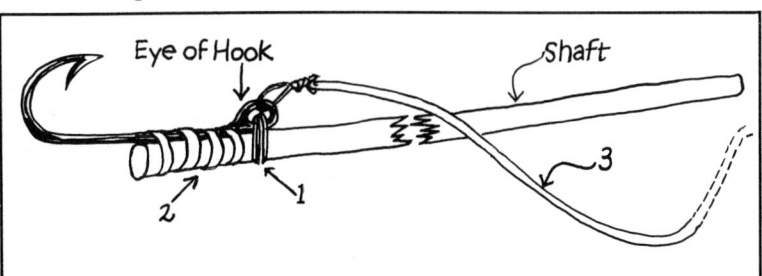

Pull the fish up and into the raft in a single, smooth pull. Pull straight back. Your gaff has no strength sideways. Throw the fish into the raft and then flop on it. Dorado especially can jump right out again. Stick your fingers in its eyes to stop it from flopping, or throw a towel or blanket over its head.

Spearfishing

If you have a speargun you are very lucky or foresightful. Remember to tie the spear to something, either the raft or your wrist. Triggerfish are not bad, but dorado get positively rude when stuck with sharp spears. If it's not tied to something, you can lose your gear.

In using your spear or speargun, you will do best if you wait until a fish is directly below you. Anywhere else, you'll have two problems. First, light refraction will make the fish look like it's somewhere it isn't, so you'll aim wrong. Second, the spear will tend to nose up when it hits the water. This is much more of a problem with a thrown spear than with a speargun.

When you pull in a speared dorado be very careful of the point, or you may have to study the section on fixing large rips in your raft. You won't be able to hold the spear away from the raft, because the dorado will be jumping around too much. Poke the point into the blanket you put on the plywood on the floor.

If you don't have a speargun or a spearhead, you can make a spear, but don't use your only knife for a tip. You cannot afford to lose it.

Trolling

If the fish are biting, this is the easiest way to catch them. It requires the least attention and allows you to use your heaviest gear. Unfortunately, the raft may not be moving fast enough to give your lures the motion they need to catch fish.

To troll, first pick a lure. If you have some of everything I listed in Chapter 13, I would suggest starting with a Scampi®. If one lure doesn't work, try another one.

If you have nothing else, cut a piece of cloth and put it on a hook. Use white or some bright color, or maybe some of each. Aluminum foil makes good lures. So do bird feathers. You can use frayed polypropylene or adhesive tape. If it's wet, it won't stick to itself. If you have enough, hang a second hook on the first one. The whole idea is to make something that looks like a meal to a fish.

Tie your lure onto the end of your heaviest line or wire, using one of the knots described above. Ideally you want to use the heaviest gear the fish will bite. Wire is stronger, but fish are more likely to bite a lure on the end of monofilament line. If you lose fish because your line is too light, go heavier. If they look at the lure but don't bite, use lighter line or pull it faster. If there are sharks around, do not use wire unless you want to be towed until it breaks.

Cut the wire or line about six feet from the lure and attach it to a swivel. Tie your heaving line to the other end of the swivel. The swivel is useful because it will allow the lure to spin in the water without weakening the line. If you have no swivels big enough to put the heaving line through, you can tie the monofilament directly to the heaving line. For trolling this is preferable to using straight monofilament because the heaving line will be much easier to pull on, especially if your hands are wet. Use what you have. And if what you have is 50 feet of monofilament, use it.

Tie the other end of the heaving line to something on the raft, preferably not yourself. If a shark or swordfish tries to eat your lure but only gets hooked in the lip, it's better for the raft to be towed around the ocean than for you to be.

Put the lure in the water and let it drift back 20 or 30 feet. Then hold on or tie it off.

If there are fish around, but they're not biting, the raft may be moving too slowly to give the lure enough action to look alive. Try pulling on the line in a jerky motion or letting it out all the way and then retrieving it quickly. If nothing bites, change lures.

Cast-and-retrieve Lures

Lures are designed with curved or slanted surfaces like airfoils. When they move through the water, they swish or jiggle or sway back and forth. If your raft is not moving fast enough to make them move, you can create the motion yourself by throwing the lure and pulling it back.

Using cast-and-retrieve lures is as simple as it sounds. Throw the lure with the line attached and pull it back in. Make sure to hold on to the bitter end or tie it to something. You would hate to throw away a lure. If one lure doesn't work, try another. If one retrieval speed doesn't work, try faster or slower, or both. If fish come up behind the lure but don't bite, try speeding up. They often will bite if they think the lure is trying to get away.

Open-ocean fish often eat flying fish, so try skipping a lure across the surface to imitate one. If the lure is heavy enough to sink, try letting it go deep and then pulling it up.

To avoid ending up with fifty or a hundred feet of loose monofilament line in your raft—which a thrashing dorado can turn into macrame—wrap the line around a pint water bottle. Swing the lure around your head and toss it, pointing the bottle outward and letting the line whiz off. It works like a primitive spinning reel. If you don't want to throw it, just let it out behind the raft. Wrap the line around the bottle as you pull it in. This makes it easy to impart a jerky motion to the lure.

If your lure stays annoyingly near the surface and nothing bites, you can put a sinker two or three feet in front of it. This is always a good idea with a feather lure. It changes the action of the feather and makes it more attractive to fish. Put a sinker near the hook to give enough weight to toss it. Try another sinker a couple of feet ahead of the hook. If you have nothing else, you can tie a silver coin onto the hook's shank to give it some flash.

If you have already caught a fish, you might use a piece of its skin instead of cloth. Better yet, if you can spare the food, cut a piece of its belly to use as a lure. It should be four to eight inches long and roughly triangular. Try to shape it so it swishes or swirls as it goes through the water. Put your hook in the skinny end. Make sure the hook goes through the skin or it will pull out of the flesh.

Fishing with Bait

After a few days you'll probably have triggerfish under the raft. They won't take any kind of lure, but they will bite a hook with a piece of fish on it. Use your smallest hook.

If you are alert and can set the hook before the fish gets it all the way inside its mouth, you will not need a wire leader. Generally fish will bite better if you don't use a leader, but they are less likely to escape if you do. Use the strongest gear the fish are stupid enough to bite.

If you see dorado around the raft, use larger hooks. Try #1/0 hooks first. Dorado are usually hungry and eager. If they turn out to be finicky, go down to #2 hooks. Start with a wire leader, and take it off if they don't bite.

Let the fish have the bait long enough to take the hook in its mouth.

If there are no fish around but scavengers, fish deeper. Put a sinker on and let the line out as far as it will go. Do not do this when there are sharks around or you'll lose your bait and hook.

Sometimes sharks are accompanied by remoras and pilot fish. They will take bait on a small hook. But be sure to make the bait small and pay attention so the shark doesn't grab it first.

If you use the flesh of the fish for bait, make sure you leave a piece of skin on it to put the hook through or the bait can fall off the hook or be stolen by scavengers.

When you are cutting bait, the intestines are obvious candidates, because you cannot eat them. You can attract fish to your bait by chumming: chop up spare fish guts and throw them in the water. This also draws sharks.

Catching Live Bait

Many fish prefer live bait. You can catch some of the tiny fish that live beneath your raft for bait.

The easiest way is to use a handy-dandy. This is four or five feet of light monofilament with several tiny hooks, each with a piece of yarn or plastic on it. Put a sinker at the end, toss it in, and jiggle it up and down. Try different depths. This will also catch fish big enough to eat.

If you have a spare bucket that you can afford to punch holes in, here's another method. Make enough holes so that water will drain out rapidly. Punch the holes inward, so there are no sharp edges on the outside.

Wire some bait, such as fish guts, into the bucket. Lower it a foot or two into the water and watch until small fish swim in after the bait. You'll have to experiment to see how fast you can lift the bucket without losing the fish.

Pulling the Fish in

When a fish takes a hook, give your line a jerk to set the hook and then pull it in. Try to do this smoothly. Do not jerk after you set the hook. If you do, the hook might tear out.

Monofilament can make nasty cuts and burns. Hold the line between the ball of your thumb and a fleshy part of your fingers. Do not hold it across a joint of your finger. Do not wrap the line around your hand. This doesn't really matter with smaller species like triggerfish or pilotfish, but it is important with medium to large dorado.

When you get the fish up to the raft, the best way to get it into the boat is with a gaff. If you don't have the means to make a gaff, and if your line is strong enough, pull the fish aboard. With small fish, just swing them in. With a trolling line, first grab the swivel with one hand. Holding the swivel will keep the line from slipping through your fingers. Grab the line near the fish with your other hand. Hold it so it runs across the fleshy parts of your fingers or use a piece of cloth or a glove. Pull the fish aboard in one motion, smoothly. The line will hold less weight in air than in water and any jerkiness adds to the stress it must endure.

If the fish is larger than you think your line will handle, grab it by the gills. This is easier said than done. You have to get the fish to lie quietly beside the raft. The fish will have to open its gills. Grab it quickly and pull it aboard. Know your fish. Tuna are not bad, but dorado take this as a strong personal affront and react violently. Some, like groupers, have sharp gill-rakers that can chew up your hand.

Killing the Fish

There are four ways to kill a fish. You can break a small fish's neck by twisting its head backwards. You can hit it in the head with a stick or knife butt. You can stick a knife through its backbone right behind the head. Or you can let it suffocate in the air.

Triggerfish can be safely held by the cheeks. They have a rough skin that gives a good grip. Watch out for the spines and teeth. You can push down the trigger (the spine that's sticking up out of the back) if you first press the spot directly in front of it. The chances are that any fish you catch trolling will be either a dorado or some member of the tuna family. You can often hold a small tuna in the air and let it dangle, quivering, until it dies. The problem with this is that it sometimes throws blood everywhere. The easiest way to hold a small tuna is by the back of the head, with your thumb and middle finger pressing in on its gill plates. For bigger ones, shift your grip upward and stick your thumb and middle finger into the eye sockets. This is an excellent grip. The fish can thrash all it wants without getting away, but most will stop all movement when you do this. Tunas have weak flesh, and it's easy to put the knife into the backbone.

Dorado are not so easy to deal with. They always go berserk. The best way to deal with dorado once it is in the raft is to try to get it onto whatever you have put in the center of the raft floor and put a blanket or shirt over its eyes. This won't be easy. Fold the cover thickly to keep the hooks out of your hand. If you have no cloth available, cover the eyes with your hand or stick your fingers in the eyes, but watch out for hooks.

The fish will quiet down very quickly after its eyes are covered. Then switch your grip from the line to the gills, which are easier to hold on to. Stick your fingers under the gill plate and up under the chin, with your fingertips nearly coming out of its mouth. Then use the point of your knife to cut the backbone, right behind the eyes. This is easiest if you lay the fish on your cleaning board.

Cutting up the Fish

Depending on how many people are in the raft, how hungry you are, and how much fish you have, you may choose to divide the fish into chunks, or you may fillet it. This makes the meat easier to apportion. It is also easier to dry anything that is left over. (Page 4 describes a fair way to divide a fish.)

In either case the best way is to begin by slitting the belly open and pulling out the innards. Save them for bait.

Skinning the Fish

First slit the skin from the anus to the tail and then on top, along one side of the dorsal fin. On the same side, cut to the bone just behind the gills and pectoral (arm) fin from top to bottom. Do the same thing at the tail. With most fish, you can now grab the skin with a pair of pliers and pull it off. Don't throw away all the skin. You may have further use for it, especially dorado skin.

Filleting

Start at the head end of the backbone and slice between the flesh and the bones that go from the spine to the dorsal fin. Slice it away an inch or two deep, and work toward the tail and deeper and deeper until you've reached the backbone for the entire length of the fish. Then start on the bottom of the fish, working from the tail toward the anus. Then lift the fillet from the tail and cut the flesh that still holds it along the spine. Now cut the meat away from the ribs. You can skip this and just cut the ribs, but you'll have to take the bones out later. Repeat the procedure for the other side of the fish.

Lay one fillet on your plywood board.

Most fish have a natural cleft between the dorsal and ventral muscles in the fillet, often with a stripe of dark meat running along it. Many fish, including dorado, have a row of small bones in this dark meat. Cut them out. Run your knife along each side. You won't throw it away, but you don't want to eat a bone by accident later.

Dry What You Don't Eat

Now cut the fillet into strips about an inch wide, half an inch to an inch thick, and four to six inches long. Cut them so the fibers run the long way.

There are two reasons for cutting them into pieces like this. First, you will have to dry what you cannot eat right away to avoid spoilage. The best way to do this is to hang the fillets up, so both sides are exposed to the air. If they are too thick, they will rot before they can dry. If the fibers don't run the long way, the pieces will fall apart when you hang them up. Thinner pieces dry much faster and they're less likely to rot, but they lose fluid faster, and fluid is probably what you need most. It's a trade off.

Pierce a small hole in one end of each piece and run a piece of string through it. Hang the pieces up to dry across the ceiling of the raft. Open both hatches to let the wind blow on the fish. If you dip the fish in salt water before hanging them up, the salt will help to desiccate it. If you don't have any string, cut the fish in thinner pieces and lay it in the open air, preferably in the sun.

Remember: the problem with dried fish is that you must have water to eat it.

Do Not Dry Tuna

Do not try to dry tuna. After a couple of hours in the sun, it becomes susceptible to scromboid poisoning (see page 46). Eat your fill and dump the rest or use it for bait.

A NOTE ON ROTTEN FISH

The flesh of most sea creatures can be dried, but the conditions on a raft are not the best for doing it. High humidity can make it rot first. The problem is telling when that has happened. You will not be able to tell by the smell, because your sense of smell will deteriorate rapidly. After a week or so, you and the fish will smell a lot alike.

Examine the fish, especially where it has been folded over. If it's green and slimy, scrape off the slime and redry it. If the tissues have begun to disintegrate, throw it away.

REFUSE

If you have to throw something overboard, check first for sharks. You don't want to encourage them. If sharks are around, wait for dark before tossing the entrails overboard.

Dangerous Creatures

SHARKS

A shark swimming around your raft probably has no idea there is food inside. It is attracted to the raft because the triggerfish and dorado that hang around are food. As long as you stay inside, it won't know you're there. If you don't dangle a foot or hand in the water, you should be all right.

Nonetheless, large sharks are a threat to you in two ways. First, they rub against things. Steve Callahan and Dougal Robertson found that sharks liked to rub the bottoms of their rafts like a cat rubbing its head on your knee. This might be interesting except that sharks have sandpaper-like skin which can rub a hole in the raft.

Second, sharks will often bite stray objects at random. I've seen them bite floating logs. A liferaft has three things that might attract a bite: barnacles on the bottom, a carbon-dioxide canister, and the lumps your body puts in the bottom. While not its normal food, barnacles can smell tasty to a hungry shark as well as to dorado and triggerfish. But the shark is likely to take a big bite rather than just a triggerfish nibble.

In some rafts, the CO_2 canister is sewn into a pocket, but in others it hangs down below the raft bottom. If a shark decides to see if it is good to eat, it can leave quite a hole in the bottom when it rips the canister away.

The same is true of your bottom. You make dents in the raft floor where you put weight on your knees, elbows, and buttocks. The dents hang deeper into the water if the floor isn't tightly inflated. So keep it pumped up.

Driving Sharks Away

You don't have to drive off every shark you see. In some waters you can count on being circled by sharks all the time. You will get used to it. The only ones you have to worry about are those close enough to rub you or bite you.

There are many stories of people who have managed to get rid of sharks, so we have many ways of doing it. But all the stories were written by survivors. We don't know if non–survivors tried the same things. Many things have worked, but nothing works all the time, except possibly a bang stick, which is a handle with a shotgun shell or a .45 round in its tip.

Hit Them on the Snout

The best way to get rid of a shark is to hit it with a paddle on the snout or on top of the head just behind the eyes. Next best is to poke it with your knife or spear. Don't stick it in past the barb, though. You really don't want to make the shark mad. And you might lose your spear.

Never splash the water near a shark. It is liable to think a small fish is in distress and attack.

If things get really hairy, you can try poking it with a lighted flare or shooting it with the flare gun. Of course, these methods won't work under water.

Cast a Bigger Shadow

Dougal Robertson says that most sharks rubbed his raft near the edges. He suggests floating blankets or something similar around the raft, to increase its shadow area hoping the sharks will continue to rub on the edges and leave the raft alone. I've never heard of this actually being done, but it's worth a try. I'd like to hear from anyone who tries it.

Shark Repellent

This is supposed to smell bad to sharks. They used to put packets of it on lifejackets. There are stories of people who used it and the sharks swam away. Other sharks swim right through clouds of it as though they don't notice it.

There is one shark repellent that works. It is made from the slime of the Moses Sole, found in the Dead Sea. It can make a shark stop in mid-bite. Unfortunately, it breaks down in a few hours. Suntan lotion manufacturers are trying to synthesize a stable version of it.

FISH THAT STING

Fish Stings in General

Fortunately, fish that are poisonous to the touch usually live on the bottom, so the only time you'll have to worry about most of them is if you wash ashore.

The pain is intense, but few people die except from stonefish and sometimes stingray wounds. In most cases, the pain lasts only a few hours, but it can be the worst pain you'll ever experience. I was once stuck by a sculpin in the tip of my index finger. I had two parallel blue lines going all the way up the inside of my arm, and my fingernail was misshapen for years.

Treatment

Do not—*repeat, do not*—use a tourniquet.

The best treatment is to put the injured part in the hottest water you can stand without injury (ideally about 112° F) for 30 minutes. Heat breaks down the poison. There is some evidence that adding Epsom salts helps. If you're on shore, build a fire and heat some water. If you're in a raft, your only source of hot water is likely to be a solar shower, and it probably won't be hot enough. If you have an extensive first-aid kit, local infiltration of procaine may help relieve the pain.

Treat the victim for shock. Elevate the feet and keep warm. This is particularly important in the case of stingray wounds. Treat the injury for infection the way you would any wound. Lacerations, such as those from stingrays, should be washed out with salt water.

Sculpin (Scorpionfish)

This is an excellent eating fish. If you catch one, hold it by grabbing its lower jaw with your thumb and index finger while it's dangling from the line. Hold it tight, so it can't flip around and stick you with the poisonous spines located on the head and fins. Cut off the spines with your nippers to prevent an accident, and fillet it very carefully. Throw the carcass away.

Sculpin (good to eat, venomous spines).

Do not handle a dead sculpin carelessly. The venom remains dangerous even after death. Also, sculpin can stay alive out of the water for up to an hour, so a sculpin that looks dead might still be able to flip up and stick you when you pick it up.

Zebrafish (Lionfish, Turkeyfish)

These are among the most beautiful fish in the ocean. If you wash ashore on or near a coral reef, you might find them in very shallow water. Zebrafish are fearless, and people are often tempted to grab one. Don't. Their poison is a lot like that of a sculpin.

Zebrafish (extremely venomous spines).

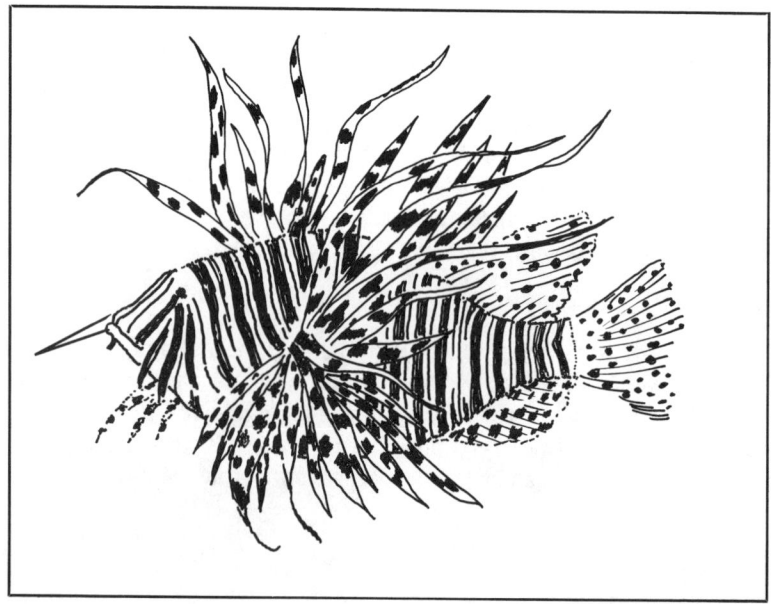

Rockfish (good to eat, mildly venomous spines).

Rockfish (Sebastes)

These are common food fish along the North American coast. They have a venom apparatus and venom similar to but not nearly as bad as a sculpin. They can be handled, but be careful. There are many species of rockfish, which vary mostly by color; the one illustrated is a generic rockfish.

Stonefish

This one can kill you. It sits in shallow water pools and looks like a rock, so it's easy to step on. Various kinds are found off India, China, Australia, the Philippines, Japan, and across the South Pacific.

Treat a stonefish wound like an ordinary fish sting. There is an antivenin, but it must be kept refrigerated between 40 and 60° F, not much help when you're adrift in a liferaft.

Stonefish (extremely venomous spines).

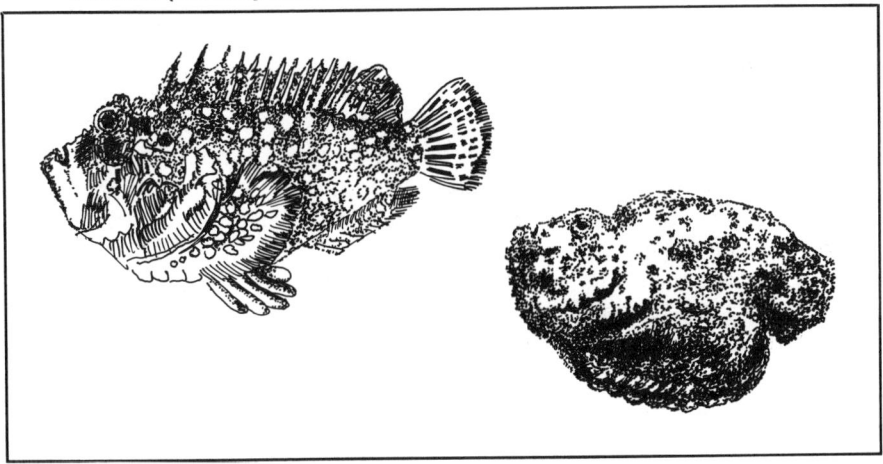

Stingrays

There are many kinds of stingrays, and they are found just about anywhere boats are. They have a barbed stinger on the tail. Some are at the base of the tail, and some are closer to the tip. They mostly live on the bottom, so they're most dangerous if stepped on. Occasionally, however, you may catch one on the surface. If there are food fish around, I would recommend cutting the line and donating the hook to the sea.

If you must eat it, try to whack the tail off with your knife before landing it or try to gaff it, throw it into the raft and stand back. Neither of these options is a very appealing prospect. If the ray lands on its back, it can slash the raft bottom.

Poisonous Sharks

A few kinds of small sharks and shark-like creatures have poisonous spines in front of their dorsal fins. Most of them live in shallow, protected water, but not all. The ratfish is supposed to live in deep water, but I have seen it caught in water 60 feet deep. The poison, pain, and treatment are like other fish stings. A few deaths have been reported, but they are rare.

Any shark-like creature with a big dorsal spine should be considered dangerous, whether or not it is poisonous.

Catfish

Only some catfish are poisonous, but it is impossible to tell by just looking. The poisonous ones inject their venom through spines at the front of the dorsal and pectoral fins, but the spines are covered with skin and look just like fins. Tropical catfish occasionally kill people. They are also pretty good eating.

Weeverfish

These are small fish that burrow in the sand or mud in the Mediterranean and North Sea and in the Atlantic from Norway to North Africa. The only time you will have to worry about them is when wading ashore or looking for food after washing ashore. They are aggressive little creatures that will attack and sting divers.

The pain is like other fish stings, but it lasts longer than most, often a full 24 hours. Infection is common, and gangrene sometimes results. Treat with heat, like other fish stings.

Moray Eels

Morays live in holes in the rocks and can be caught on hook and line by the luckless. They lack venom glands, but the slime around their mouths seems to be poisonous. Wounds from moray bites fester and do not heal easily.

Sea Snakes

Sea snakes are the most abundant reptile, with about fifty species. During the breeding season, they are sometimes seen in enormous spherical masses, with hundreds of snakes doing whatever it is snakes do when they get together. They have been seen migrating in hordes ten feet wide and as long as 60 miles.

Sea snakes live anywhere the water is warm and in some cold places as well, usually within a couple of hundred miles of shore. They feed on the bottom, but they have to come to the surface to breathe, although they can stay down for hours at a time. Most are three to four feet long, but some species grow as long as nine feet.

Some sea snakes can be extremely docile at times. At other times, the same species may become aggressive. Some species seem to be aggressive all the time. Occasionally, they will bite a hook and line. If they do, cut the line and donate the hook.

The poison is extremely powerful. It is more toxic than king cobra venom. It is neurotoxic, myotoxic, and hemotoxic. One drop has enough poison in it to kill three grown men. Some kinds of snakes can inject as much as eight drops in a single bite. They inject the venom with small fangs of the cobra type. They usually have two fangs on each side.

Symptoms usually develop slowly, taking anywhere from 20 minutes to several hours to emerge. An hour is common. But sea snake bites are deceptive. Often, the site of the bite shows no damage and it is difficult to associate the symptoms with the bite.

Symptoms vary. They may start with aching and anxiety or with mild euphoria. Drooping of the eyelids is common, as is generalized aching, stiffness and weakness of the muscles. The tongue feels thick and it may be hard to talk. Paralysis starts in the legs and advances up to the torso, arms, and neck. The pulse becomes weak and irregular. There may be nausea, vomiting, spasms, twitching, dry, burning throat and heavy thirst.

A sea-snake bite is definitely life-threatening. About a third of the victims die. The symptoms worsen: the skin becomes cold, clammy, and blue; convulsions begin and grow increasingly severe; breathing becomes difficult. The victim lapses into unconsciousness and dies.

Treatment: Not much can be done in a liferaft. The victim should lie down, keeping the wound below the level of the heart. Restrict the movement of the wounded limb, and avoid all exertion. Keep the victim warm and as calm as possible. Drinking water is okay, but no alcohol is allowed.

STINGING INVERTEBRATES

The treatment is essentially the same for wounds caused by all stinging invertebrates:

1. Remove whatever is causing the injury.
2. Give the victim two acetaminophen tablets.
3. If the patient has trouble breathing, inject .05 ml of 1:1000 Epinephrin hydrochloride subcutaneously.

Jellyfish

Treat all jellyfish as poisonous. A couple of hundred kinds of jellyfish can sting you, but only a few are really dangerous. The difficulty lies in learning which ones are which. The best policy is to stay away from all of them.

Symptoms range from a prickling rash and blisters to muscular cramps, nausea, vomiting, backache, loss of speech, diminished sense of touch and temperature, frothing at the mouth, respiratory problems, paralysis, delirium, convulsions and death.

The obvious way to avoid being stung is to stay out of the water. Be especially careful when water is thrown into the raft in rough weather: it can carry jellyfish with it. Stay alert for jellyfish when you are wading through shallows approaching shore.

Treatment: First pull the jellyfish off. They have millions of venom-injecting cells called nematocysts on their tentacles, and these cells keep firing as long as the tentacles are in contact with the body. Use gloves, a stick, seaweed, a piece of cloth or paper, anything to avoid touching the tentacles with your bare hands. Lifeguards in Australia wear pantyhose while dragging for jellyfish, because the nematocysts cannot penetrate the nylon mesh.

Robert Hartwick, of James Cook University in Townsville, Australia, discovered that pouring vinegar over the tentacles neutralizes the unfired nematocysts. Then you can pull the tentacles off easily.

Treatment depends on what you have available. In a liferaft this usually means not much. Of all the things you are likely to have on a liferaft, alcohol (drinking or rubbing) is the best. Pour it over the skin or pat it on with a wet cloth. This dilutes the venom and reduces the amount that actually gets into your system. *Do not* apply alcohol before the tentacles have been removed. Alcohol causes the nematocysts to fire, injecting more poison into the victim.

If you have a complete first-aid kit, antihistamine pills and topical creams may help the rash. Otherwise, use diluted ammonium hydroxide, olive oil, sugar, diluted ammonia, or papain (meat tenderizer). Some people say they have been helped by applying onion juice or strong black tea.

Morphine will relieve the pain.

Intravenous calcium gluconate has been recommended for control of muscular spasms.

Be prepared to give CPR if needed.

Corals

Coral cuts heal very slowly. The danger is partly from laceration and partly from poison. The skeleton of some coral is like a razor mace; it has little knives sticking out in every direction, and it can slash you terribly. The creatures which make up the corals range from harmless to moderately poisonous, but the climate in which corals thrive— hot and humid—is also good for bacteria, so cuts often become infected and take a long time to heal.

Ordinarily all you can or need do is clean the wound promptly, washing out all the sand and random organic materials that always seem to be in a coral wound. You may want to put an antiseptic ointment on it. If it gets bad, have the victim lie down, with the injured place (usually a foot or hand) elevated. You can give antihistamine pills or ointment.

You will have to worry about coral stings only when you're washing ashore.

Cones

If you wash ashore in the tropics and look for seashells for food or for souvenirs, watch out for these. They are the only kind of seashell that is really dangerous to touch. They range from half an inch to several inches long and can stick you through a pocket or gloves.

Symptoms start with a burning around the wound, followed by numbness and tingling, which may spread over the whole body but especially to the lips and mouth. In bad cases, the victim may be paralyzed. There is usually no problem breathing. Death, when it occurs, is usually from cardiac failure.

The symptoms often worsen for about six hours. If you live through this, you will probably recover within 24 hours, though the site of the wound may take a few weeks to heal fully.

Treatment: The patient should rest. Be prepared to administer CPR. Do not give any respiratory depressants. Respiratory stimulants are probably useless because the cone venom blocks their action.

There is no antivenin for cone stings.

Bristleworms

If you see a segmented worm with white spines, do not touch it. The spines will come off in your hand like slivers of glass. They are sometimes found in floating seaweed. Stings from the bristles can cause several days of inflammation, itching, swelling, and numbness. The numbness may last for weeks. They also bite.

The best way of removing the bristles is to apply adhesive tape and pull them off. On the beach you can rub the area with sand. Apply alcohol, lotions, or local anaesthetic cream or ointment for pain. You may need to give antihistamines or antibiotics or apply steroid creams.

Cone shells (venomous).

CONTINUING
MEDICAL CARE

We have dealt with fish stings and other animal injuries in Chapter 7, eating poisonous fish in Chapter 6, and bleeding, CPR, drowning, hypothermia, broken bones, and shock in Chapter 3. There remain a few conditions which we must be aware of, including conditions which existed before you and your companions were forced to take to the liferaft. As captain, make sure you are aware of any special medical conditions among your crew.

PRESCRIPTION DRUGS

Do not continue to take prescription medicines while in the liferaft unless not taking them would be life-threatening.

Do continue to take digitalis, epilepsy drugs (other than barbiturates), cortisone-like drugs, or nitroglycerine.

If you don't have enough water going through your system, drugs will not act the way they are supposed to and neither will your body. If you have a watermaker or enough water to drink your normal three quarts a day, go ahead and take your medicine.

DEHYDRATION

Unless you have a watermaker, dehydration can be a factor in just about all of the medical problems that can come up after a few days in the raft. It can cause some and make others worse. Anyone who has been been on water rationing will be weaker than usual, and you cannot expect the same strength or endurance from yourself or from the crew as you would aboard ship. After a month or more on a raft, you probably won't be able to walk when you wash ashore or get rescued, unless you've had plenty of water. If you have enough water, you can get through just about anything.

Salt and Dehydration:

People who have survived drowning still risk dying of dehydration. The raging thirst arises from the body's need to get rid of all the sodium it has taken in. It does this does by increasing urination. The same thing happens to people who drink sea water. If there is not enough water to replace what they urinate, they may die. Slow salt build-up is likely if you eat seaweed, drink rainwater captured off the canopy, or rely on a solar still.

The only way to treat salt build-up is to drink a lot of fresh water and urinate it away. You can do this during a rainstorm after the water jugs are full, but remember the initial necessity of limiting water to trigger the body's water-retention mechanisms.

FROSTBITE

This occurs when tissues are destroyed by freezing, usually from exposure to cold air. Damage occurs to a larger area than the part that is actually frozen. It usually starts with fingers, toes, cheeks, nose, or ears. It may spread up the arms and legs.

The skin looks white or greyish yellow because of ice crystals in the skin. There may be pain at first, but it may go away, leaving only a feeling of being very cold and numb. There may be tingling or aching.

If you press a frostbitten area with only surface damage, the surface will feel hard, but it will yield a little because of the unfrozen tissue underneath. A bad frostbite will feel frozen hard. Blisters will occur within 12 to 36 hours. When it thaws, it will be red and swollen. Then gangrene sets in, and the tissue dies.

Treatment: In theory you should not try to thaw a hard frostbite until you get to a place where they can do it right. Unless you are close to land or heavily travelled sea-lanes, you do not have much choice, but do not rush to thaw it out.

Shallow frostbite should always be warmed immediately, to keep it from getting worse. Breathe on a small spot or put your hand over the affected area. Put the victim's frostbitten hands in someone else's armpits or inside their clothes. Change armpits from time to time, so the heat-givers stay warm.

After the frozen part is warmed up, wash it with soap and fresh water, if you have it. Be careful not to pop any blisters.

Keep the rewarmed part elevated.

If you have gauze bandages, place them between fingers and toes to keep them separated.

Do not massage.

Do not apply any ointments or creams.

Do not give the patient any alcohol, because it affects the way the blood circulates and can cause a loss in body heat.

Ten mg of Morphine Sulphate may be injected intramuscularly for pain, *but only if you get medical advice by radio to do so. Do not do it on your own*, because morphine is a respiratory depressant. If you do, be alert for slow or shallow breathing, and be ready to give CPR.

Do not let it happen again. Frostbite is worse the second time around.

CHILBLAINS

This occurs when the temperature is above freezing, up to about 60° F. It mostly affects the shins and the back of the hands.

The skin swells and becomes bluish red. The skin often itches and burns, which rewarming may make worse.

If the condition is not too bad, it may just go away. If you get it too often, it will build up to chronic swelling, deep purple skin discoloration, blisters, and bleeding lesions that heal slowly and leave blotchy scars.

Treatment: Warm the affected area, possibly by breathing on it. Do not massage it. Apply petrolatum or a similar ointment.

IMMERSION FOOT (TRENCH FOOT)

This condition occurs when the foot is exposed to cold sea water (between 32° and 50° F) for long periods. Inactivity, bad diet, and tight or wet clothing can help bring it on.

Symptoms include swelling of the tissues involved, numbness, tingling, itching, pain, cramps, and skin discoloration. There probably won't be any blistering or tissue destruction unless something else is wrong.

Prevention: Stay warm and dry when the water is cold. Sponge the raft dry. Wear plastic bags or rags over socks. Wiggle and move your feet to keep blood circulating.

Treatment: Get warm and dry and stay warm and dry. Apply petrolatum for skin discomfort.

HEATSTROKE

This is a life-threatening emergency. It results when the body's heat regulation systems break down. Most heat loss comes from evaporation of perspiration, so a breakdown in the sweat system can bring it on.

The onset of heatstroke is abrupt. Early symptoms may include headache, excessive warmth, and generally feeling lousy. The victim's skin is typically dry, flushed and hot, with no sweat. (If sweat is present, it was probably generated before the heatstroke came on.) Being hot but not sweating is a sign of heatstroke, so everyone should be on the lookout for the symptoms. If someone stops sweating when the temperature is high, start treatment quickly.

As it develops, heatstroke symptoms may include:

— Fainting, delirium or convulsion
— Small hemorrhages or spots on the skin
— Strong, rapid pulse, often over 160 beats per minute
— Slightly elevated blood pressure
— Deep, rapid breathing
— Pupils at first contracted, then dilated
— There may be muscular twitching, cramps, and projectile vomiting, sometimes followed by circulatory collapse and deep shock.

Core body temperature is frequently higher than 106° F and not uncommonly over 108° F. This is a bad sign.

Treatment: Take immediate steps to lower the body temperature. Undress the victim and sponge with seawater. Cover with cold packs or wet blankets. Massage the skin to stimulate blood flow. Take the temperature every 10 minutes until it falls below 101°F (38.3°C).

After the body temperature drops, the patient must rest for several days in the coolest part of the raft. Do what you can to direct the breeze onto the patient. Keep track of the body temperature. If it starts to rise, go through the cooling routine again.

Do *not* give the patient morphine sulphate, epinephrine, or stimulants. Administer sedatives only to control convulsions.

COMPARISON OF HEAT STROKE, HEAT EXHAUSTION, AND SHOCK

	Heat Stroke	Heat Exhaustion	Shock
Pulse	strong & rapid	weak & rapid	weak & rapid
Pupils	first contracted, then dilated	dilated	
Skin	flushed, hot & dry	pale & sweaty	pale, cool & damp
Breathing	deep & rapid	shallow & rapid	shallow & rapid
Other Symptoms	muscular twitching cramps convulsions vomiting slightly elevated blood pressure	weakness dizziness mild muscular cramps nausea blurred vision	faintness dizziness other trauma: broken bones or bleeding
Treatment	sponge with sea water wet blankets massage	lie down give water loosen clothing rest	lie down with feet up keep warm water—if no head or stomach wound rest

HEAT EXHAUSTION

The body regulates its temperature through the blood supply. To lose heat, more blood is sent to the surface and it is cooled by the evaporation of sweat from the skin. In heat*stroke* the system stops operating; you have no sweat to cool the skin. With heat *exhaustion*, the system keeps working but overloads. Too much blood becomes pooled near the skin, and the heart and brain are starved for oxygen. The capillaries constrict in reaction to this shortage, and the skin turns bloodless and pale.

The victim will sweat heavily and have a fast, weak pulse. The pupils will be dilated, and the breathing will be rapid and shallow. There may be weakness, dizziness, nausea, dim or blurred vision, or mild muscular cramps.

Treatment: If your raft is the type that lets you sit on the flotation chambers, first put the victim in a sitting position with the head lowered to the knees. Then move him in a reclining position, on the back with the knees drawn up. Don't put anything under the head. Loosen tight clothing to make it easier for surface blood to flow.

Ordinary treatment calls for the patient to slowly sip a pint of cool water with one teaspoon of table salt or crushed salt tablets added. Intake should amount to four ounces every 15 minutes for an hour. Stop if vomiting occurs. The patient should rest for a few days.

In a liferaft, water is probably limited. Salt can be dangerous, depending on how long you have been in the raft and how much water you have and expect to have. Do not put salt into your system if you don't have enough water to flush it out. If you decide to add salt, you can crush salt tablets from your first-aid kit.

If you have water but no salt, add a tablespoon of sea water to a pint of fresh water. This is a rare therapeutic use for a very small amount of sea water, diluted to one part in 64. This does not mean you can drink sea water just because you're thirsty. You must not use sea water to extend your supply of fresh water.

HEAT CRAMPS

Heat cramp is more painful but less dangerous than heatstroke or heat exhaustion. It is a cramping of the abdominal or skeletal muscles due to loss of salts through sweating. It is most common in the muscles that bend the arms and legs. If the victim has drunk a lot of fresh water without replacing the salts, the condition can be much worse, severe enough to make the victim scream. If untreated, heat cramps can last several hours but are not considered dangerous and will go away by themselves. Blood pressure will remain normal and rectal temperature will run about 98°-100° F (36.6°-37.7° C).

Treatment: Move the victim to the coolest spot in the raft and sponge with salt water. Give the patient water with one teaspoon table salt or crushed salt tablets per pint. Allow four ounces to start with and four ounces every fifteen minutes for an hour, or until the symptoms go away. Massage may help the muscle pain.

In a liferaft, the fresh water supply is limited. If supplies are short, remember that heat cramps are very painful but not fatal. Regarding salt, the same problem exists as with heat exhaustion, and I'll repeat what I said there. Salt can be dangerous, depending on how long you have been in the raft and how much water you have and expect to have. Do not put salt into your system if you don't have enough water to flush it out.

SUNBURN

Sunburn is preventable, and there is no reason to die of it or to make your stay in the raft any more uncomfortable than it already is.

Prevent sunburn by keeping covered. Stay under the canopy. Watchstanders should wear hats and sunscreen when sticking their heads out into the hot sun. Everyone should wear sunglasses whenever looking outside during the daytime.

SALT-WATER BOILS

If you are adrift in the raft for a few weeks, you will probably develop salt-water boils on your buttocks, knees, elbows, and hands. They are caused by the constant rubbing on the wet raft floor. They are very painful, especially when something touches them.

To prevent them, keep the raft dry and regularly apply some sort of oil or barrier cream to your skin in the areas that touch the raft.

Once the boils appear, there is not much you can do to treat them. Do not wear clothes over the sores; wash them in fresh water or rainwater; gently rub on some oil or cream, and try to keep them clean. They take a long time to heal, but the pain will stop if you can keep them salt-free for 48 hours.

Do not squeeze the pus. This will hinder healing.

ALIMENTARY PROBLEMS

Castaways often go for long periods without bowel movements. One reported case went 30 days without one. When it finally came, it left him dizzy, but he suffered no long-term consequences.

It is easy to get constipated on a liferaft. There is not much to eat, so there's not much waste. Your diet is primarily raw fish, which is mostly protein. Further, you don't have enough water to wash things through, so they pack up.

Seaweed can provide the bulk necessary for good functioning of the gut, but only if you have to have enough water to rinse the salt off and to wash it through.

When constipation becomes painful, it is time for an enema. Lacking a hot-water bottle or enema bag, you can use any container to which you can attach a rubber hose or tube. Lay the patient face-down, with one knee drawn up. Lubricate the tip of the tubing and insert it about three inches into the rectum. Do this gently; you may be next.

For lubrication, you can use fresh water, or turtle oil, or even storm oil from the sea anchor, but do not use salt water. It's just like drinking sea water, and just as dangerous. Some salt will be left behind to be absorbed into the system.

LOSS OF MUSCLE TONE

This is inevitable, though it can be limited by doing isometric exercises. Push one arm against the other or one leg against someone else's. It takes a lot of repetitions to do any good, but it's worth the effort, and you will have plenty of time.

Perform isometrics when it's cool, so you don't waste sweat. And don't do it at all if the water supply is low.

SCURVY

This comes from a lack of vitamin C. Some people have been deprived of vitamin C for months without noticeable problems. Others have shown symptoms after six weeks. Symptoms include bleeding gums and red hemorrhagic pustules.

Treatment: Consume some vitamin C. This can be found in plankton, some seaweeds, and, of course, in pill form.

THE LIFERAFT

CHOOSING A LIFERAFT

Liferafts vary a great deal from manufacturer to manufacturer and between a manufacturer's different rafts. All raft-makers would love to tell you all about their rafts, at a showroom, at a boat show, or by mail. Let them. It's a good way to learn.

Here are some features to look for:

Inflation Tubes

A raft should be inflatable, with a canopy. Nearly all are. If you are going out on the ocean, your raft should have two main inflation tubes. These may be arranged with one on top of the other or one inside the other. Each tube should have enough buoyancy to support all the raft's intended inhabitants. Some coastal-service rafts have only one tube.

Tubes should be at least twelve inches in diameter to avoid bending. Gas expands as the temperature rises, so every inflation chamber should have at least one pressure relief valve. Otherwise the amount of gas necessary to inflate the raft at 50°F could explode it at 100°F.

Some rafts are inflated with pure carbon dioxide. In very cold weather, these inflate slowly and sometimes not fully. To solve this problem, some manufacturers mix in nitrogen, which has a much lower boiling point than CO_2, so it inflates quickly and fully.

Single or Double Floor

To protect you from the cold, most ocean-service rafts have double floors, which you inflate with the hand pump. The top and bottom materials join at seams, which collect the water that inevitably comes in the hatch. Water will also concentrate where you sit.

Some rafts use a single built-in floor and have a separate air mattress to keep you insulated frcm the ocean and above the water in the raft. Others have a single floor and include blow-up drop-stitch pads to sit on. These are made of two pieces of fabric sewn into a flat pillow with numerous seams to inhibit air circulation within the pillow and improve the insulation value. Both kinds of pad will work. The people who make them say they work better than a built-in double floor. I haven't found any real studies on insulation values, but not sitting in water is a definite benefit.

Stability

A liferaft consisting only of a couple of big inner-tubes and a canopy would be extremely easy to capsize. If the center of gravity shifted when the raft was tipped by a wave, the wind could catch the edge and flip it right over. Modern liferafts use three devices to avoid this: inflated overhead arches, sea anchors, and ballast systems.

Arches

All covered rafts have at least one inflatable arch. Two arches (or three) are better than one, because they will keep the waves off you better in a heavy sea, and they make the raft easier to right if you capsize.

Sea Anchor

A sea anchor (in conjunction with ballast pockets) has been shown to keep a liferaft from tipping over in some hellish seas, but it is not a perfect answer. A sea anchor is designed to protect you from waves coming from the same direction as the wind. But while there will always be waves coming from the direction of a high wind, they will often come from other directions as well. If these are big enough and timed right, they can roll you right over in spite of the ballast pockets. This is not as common as some raft-makers claim, because the wind is a bigger factor in capsizing liferafts than waves. But it not as uncommon as others claim, either. The rafts should right themselves, but the experience would be unpleasant at the very least and possibly life-threatening.

Sea anchors also vary a great deal in quality from raft to raft. Some look more like plankton nets, a foot in diameter and made of panty-hose nylon. Others are three or four feet across and sturdy. Examine the equipment photographs in the manufacturer's advertising brochure. In general, stronger is better. Bigger is also better, if you have room for it.

Ballast Systems

Ballast systems consist of plastic bags under the liferaft. The bags fill with water and resist being lifted out of the water by the wind if an edge is lifted by a wave.

Some rafts have two to four small pockets placed 90° or 180° apart. British tests performed in Iceland showed that rafts with a few small pockets are insufficiently stable in heavy weather, so most raft-makers now use larger pockets. Some are arranged in a circle all around the raft with small air spaces between them. The new pockets are also deeper. They have a triangular cross-section, weighted along the center seam so as to open quickly.

One liferaft manufacturer has patented a ballast pocket which goes all the way around the raft. This fills with water at the top but prevents the water from circulating within the tube, so the tipping moment is maintained if the edge of the raft is lifted clear of the surface. In a high wind there is some risk that such a pocket will itself become part of the sail area and thus increase the chance of capsizing.

Another maker has patented a "hemispherical" system using one enormous ballast pocket. This underwater bag is about the same size as the canopy, divided into two sections with freeing ports between them. In severe weather, rafts using this are more stable than other rafts. If the sea anchor breaks loose, they are infinitely safer and harder to tip over in heavy weather. If the sea anchor remains in place, the difference is less striking.

This type of raft is also less affected by the wind than the current, which means that it will maintain your position better but take a bigger beating from wind-blown waves.

Although this particular design is patented, the benefit from large ballast pockets has been well enough demonstrated that we can assume other manufacturers will design something similar, if only making their old pockets bigger.

A disadvantage of the hemispherical system is that you can't sail it. If you are in the trade winds, you may well want to sail downwind to the doldrums in search of rain. In liferafts with conventional ballast pockets you can empty the pockets and trip or haul in the sea anchor to sail faster than the current. At present, you cannot do that with a hemispherical system, although there is no reason the manufacturer could not design a way to empty the bag.

Materials

Rafts are usually made of a synthetic rubber bonded to nylon. Synthetic is preferred to natural. Natural rubber floats, stretches, and bends well enough, but degrades quicker than synthetics.

Neoprene is the most common synthetic rubber used today. Higher grade neoprene has a loose-woven fiber impregnated in it, which makes it harder to rip. You can check whether a particular raft uses this grade of material by rubbing a wet finger on it. Better neoprene will show little squares of fiber.

The disadvantage of neoprene for a manufacturer is that it cannot be electronically welded or heat-sealed. It must be glued, which costs more. Still, most rafts are glued. A glued raft is much easier to repair. Furthermore, it can be repaired in many more ports. Butyl is sometimes used instead of neoprene, because it stands up to cold and to abrasion better. Urethane weighs less than neoprene, withstands abrasion well, and can be heat-sealed or electronically welded. It also costs more.

Hatches should close with nylon zippers or tie-downs. Velcro® is a wonderful invention, but it isn't strong enough to withstand waves pounding on it.

Color is important. The interior should not be orange. When the wind starts flapping an orange canopy, people inside can get seasick or dizzy. Blue is much more calming.

Size

Rafts are rated for the number of people they can hold, not the number they can hold comfortably. It should be big enough to hold everyone you might have to, but not much bigger. If it is too big, it will be hard to keep warm with only body heat, especially in high latitudes. In the tropics, the occupants will appreciate the extra room if you get the next size larger. Whether you can stretch out in it is a factor in deciding between different small rafts. Six-person rafts vary between six- and eight-foot outside diameter. If you have to spend any time at all in the raft, there should be room enough for at least one person at a time to lie down flat. If you cannot, after a while your joints will ache and it will be harder to crawl ashore when you reach land.

Shape

Oblong rafts are easier to lie down in. Manufacturers of the round ones claim they are more stable in a rolling sea because they don't allow the forces of the sea to be concentrated on one spot. Makers of oblong rafts say that's not true. I would buy a round one.

One manufacturer makes a raft shaped like a sailboat, which is an interesting idea, but the one I saw was lake-equipped rather than ocean-equipped, and it was orange inside.

Canister or Valise

If you are deciding between a valise-type and a canister-type, get the canister unless you can stow it in a place where it will stay dry but remain accessible in an emergency. Small-boat emergencies often occur suddenly and having the raft stowed on the outside of the vessel is important. You may not have time to get it from under the seat in the galley.

A fiberglass canister will last longer than one made of ABS plastic. The cradle should be made of aluminum or stainless steel.

MAINTAINING A LIFERAFT ABOARD SHIP

Repacking your liferaft from time to time is essential, and it must be done by professionals. Like packing a parachute, it must be done right or it will not work. And, like packing a parachute, you only get one chance.

As captain, all you have to do is kick the hydrostatic release once a month to check it, and send the raft in to be repacked at the interval stamped on its tag, probably once a year. And keep the deckhand from painting it.

MAINTAINING A LIFEBOAT ABOARD SHIP

If you have lifeboats, one officer should be assigned to make sure they are ready for use at all times. By law, this includes:

Checking the equipment once a month to make sure it is complete;
Checking the winch control apparatus at least every three months—
check motor controllers, emergency switches, master switches, and limit switches; remove any drain plugs; run the lifeboat out on its davits;
Making sure that lifeboat decks are clear of cargo or other obstructions which would hamper launching;
Testing lifeboat motors at least five minutes forward and five minutes reverse once a week;

Stripping, cleaning, and overhauling the whole thing once a year;
Changing the fuel once a year.

This maintenance may be performed at sea provided you have
enough lifeboats on each side to accommodate everyone on the vessel.

MAINTAINING A LIFERAFT IN USE

Modern, Coast Guard-approved liferafts are well designed and well made.
The current record for consecutive accidental days in an inflatable raft is
118, set in 1972 by Maurice and Maralyn Bailey. Their raft is said to have
been in good shape at the end except for two things. A fish punctured the
bottom tube, which they never could repair, and the tape joining the tubes
eventually came loose, which caused them to ship water.

Steve Callahan floated 76 days in a raft guaranteed for just 30 days.
His only problem with the raft came when he stuck a hole in it with a
spear attached to an angry dorado. He had to jury rig a plug which held
after some difficulty, and he stayed afloat.

On the other hand, the Robertsons had to abandon their raft for
their dinghy on the seventeenth day. It had been disintegrating under
them for days from many small abrasions. In particular, the tripper line to
the ballast pocket under their raft was too short and wore a hole in the
flotation chamber. Check all such lines.

The Robertsons also found wear in the fabric on the bottom of the
raft, where the floor attaches to the flotation chamber. This allowed sea
water into the raft in spite of constant sponging and bailing. This
contributed to the formation of salt-water boils, which are particularly
unpleasant things to have.

Their pump didn't work, so they had to inflate the raft by blowing on
a piece of tubing without a mouthpiece. It got to be an every hour
pump-up until the raft finally got too bad to keep, and the whole group
took to the dinghy.

Punctures

The liferaft accident that can happen quickest and with the least warning
is a puncture by knife or spear. Prevent this by requiring that all pointed
tools be sheathed or wrapped up at all times except when actually in use.

If you have a trident, keep styrofoam on the tips or wrap it in a shirt or another article of clothing. Do not leave fish hooks lying loose on the floor of the raft.

When you gather up loose gear from the wreck or find things floating by, don't tie anything hard or sharp to the raft. Instead, tie it to the sea anchor line. Prepare a pad on which to flop a captured fish so spear or hooks cannot poke holes in the raft.

Abrasion

Though not as quick as knives and spears, abrasion can make holes just as big. The materials in the flotation chamber are intended to withstand certain temperatures and pressures. They are not designed to withstand abrasion. So whenever you attach something to a raft, make sure to use chafing gear (a wrapped rag) and check it regularly. Do not rig a sail or a tow-line which allows any line or spar to touch the flotation chambers directly. Pad it. If it touches the rubber, it can rub through in a week or two.

Keep the raft pumped up. This will reduce wear.

Sharks, Dorados and Turtles

Castaways tell of sharks and dorados bumping the bottoms of their rafts, possibly eating barnacles off the raft bottom. They were naturally concerned about abrasion.

Dougal Robertson observed that sharks bumped him more often near the edge of the raft than in the middle. In his book *Sea Survival: A Manual*, he suggests floating blankets or whatever else is available to increase the perimeter of the raft. The object is to increase the shadow area and encourage sharks to continue to strike the edges, sparing the raft and its occupants. I have never heard of it being tried in the real world, but it sure seems worth a try.

Another way of dealing with sharks is to hit them with a paddle on the snout or on top of the head just behind the eyes.

Turtles bite rafts, probably to eat barnacles off the bottom, possibly as an invitation to sex. They are less bothered than sharks by a whack on the nose or on the shell. If you grab a turtle and hold it by the hind flippers for a little while, it will go away. If you grab it by the hind flippers and pull it into the raft, it will stay for dinner.

REPAIRING HOLES

Fix holes quickly, before they get too big to fix. To repair a hole on the inside of the raft, try the patch kit first. Follow the directions, which will probably be to make sure the area is clean, dry, and lightly abraded; spread the glue evenly on the area around the hole and on a patch that is at least an inch bigger than the damage in every direction. Wait until it dries, then put a second coat on. When the second coat is tacky, put the patch in the damaged area. Give it at least 24 hours to dry before inflating the raft hard.

One liferaft manufacturer told me that the repair kit they include in their raft was "very difficult to use unless (you have) relatively calm and dry conditions." Good luck.

To fix a big hole, any hole on the outside of the raft, or one inside that you have not been able to fix with a patch, use a plug or a clamp.

Fixing Holes with Plugs

The proper kind of plug is notched all along its length. This is to provide a coarse surface to press the rubber into. If you don't have the proper kind of plug, use anything you can tie string around: a screwdriver, a block of wood, a rolled-up piece of rubber, a bolt. If you use wood, carve a notch around it to press the rubber into.

To use a plug, stick the pointed end in the hole and gather some material around it and secure it with a clamp or tie it tight with string, not wire. Wire will cut the rubber. The pressure will tend to roll the string over the top of the plug. If the knot does not use up all the stretch in the line, it may roll until the stretch is filled with the increasing diameter of the plug. If this happens, you will lose some of what you gather, so gather plenty and tie it as tight as you can.

Fixing Holes with Clamps

Some rafts come with clamps for fixing holes. These consist of two alumimum plates with rubber gaskets around them. One plate goes inside the inflation tube, and the other goes outside. Screw them together tight with the wing-nut. This is intended to be a temporary repair, until you can make a permanent patch.

SAILS

One brand of liferaft comes with a sail and steering oars. Another can be rigged to sail downwind. Unless the raft is designed for it, a sail is harder to rig on a liferaft than on a lifeboat, but it is possible. You can use a spare blanket, a piece of canvas, a sheet of plastic, or even clothing, if you can tie enough together. If it comes to it—and if you're close to land and won't be needing the shade or warmth—you might be able to cut a flap in the canopy and use it as a sail. A sail doesn't have to be pretty to work.

Yards and masts will be harder to come by. If you have them, you can use oars or bits of floating lumber.

In principle, three kinds of sail (and variations) are possible on a liferaft: square with a central mast and horizontal yard, triangular with a vertical mast and horizontal yard, or square with two vertical yards and no mast. On sailing vessels, a triangular sail is more efficient across the wind, but a liferaft cannot sail well enough for you to tell the difference. Rig what you can with what you have.

In practice, the easiest to make and use will probably be a squarish sail with more or less vertical yards. To make it, stick your yards (oars, spars, sticks, gaffs) out the hatch.

Types of sails possible on an inflatable raft.

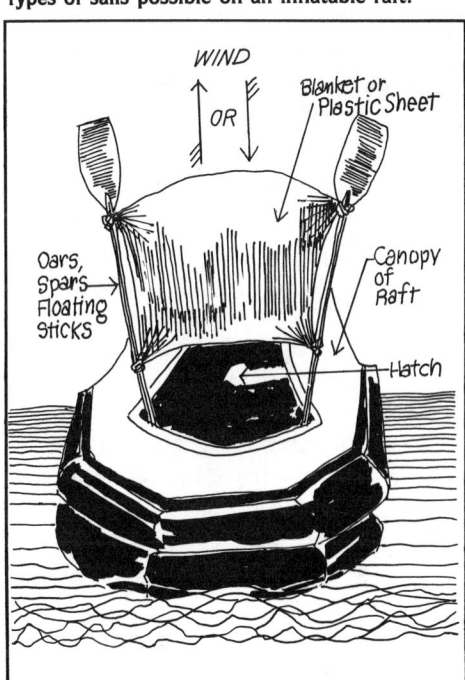

Be extremely careful about preventing spars, oars, and lines from touching the flotation chambers. They can rub through in a week. Use chafing gear or tie them someplace else. Tie a shirt or something similar where the spars touch the raft bottom, and move them from time to time, checking the rubber underneath.

Do not rig the sail so tight that it is stretched flat. Let it billow; it will be more efficient. The motive power of a sail comes partly from the wind pushing on one side but mostly from the vacuum the shape of the sail creates on the downwind side. A flat sail creates too much turbulence and provides too little pull.

Try to rig your sail higher than the canopy. If you cannot, a lower sail will still help you go faster in the direction the wind is blowing because it will catch the wind better than the raft, but you won't be able to sail off the wind very well.

SAILING ACROSS THE WIND

The sails you are likely to be able to make on a liferaft will push you mostly straight downwind. Without them you would move in the same direction, although not as quickly. If your destination does not lie downwind, it is possible to sail slightly across the wind, but don't expect too much. A liferaft is not a high-performance vessel.

To sail across the wind, you must have a keel. Otherwise, when you turn the sail away from the wind, it will spin the raft until it is square again.

RUDDER AND KEEL

The sea anchor is a kind of keel, although not much of one. With your sea anchor streaming, if you turn your sail diagonally to the wind, you will head slightly off the wind. The effect won't be great, but it may help if you need to make a few degrees change in course.

If you empty and secure all the ballast pockets except the one in the stern, its drag will orient you to the wind.

You might try tying a fish-cleaning board to a paddle to use as a steering oar or rudder in conjunction with the sea anchor. Or you might use one in front as a keel and one in back as a rudder. Be very careful not to abrade the raft. Place folded cloth between the paddle and the flotation chamber.

Be sure to take your paddles in during rough weather or when sharks are around. Sharks bite things. If you have to spend much time in the raft, you will find the boards will be more important to you for cleaning fish than as rudders and keels.

The wind will usually push you faster than the water whether you have a sail or not. This means there is usually an apparent current running beneath you, so with or without a sail, the paddle/fish cleaning board technique might be considered at any time.

PADDLES

Rafts are designed to drift slowly, which means they are very hard to paddle. Furthermore, rowing or paddling uses a great deal of energy. Do it only if you are so close to land that it will not take long to get there. If you must paddle any distance, try to do it at night, so the paddlers will lose less water through sweat. The easiest way is to trip and haul in the sea anchor and have one paddler at each entrance. Before you start, empty the ballast pockets or you will find yourself rowing against the ocean.

TYING RAFTS TOGETHER

If your party occupies more than one raft, tie the rafts together. They are not, however, designed for the stress of a line constantly jerking from the side, so the point of attachment may weaken or pull loose. Check the tie-point frequently, and switch from place to place if you see damage starting.

One way to reduce the damage from the rafts surging apart is to make the line as long as possible and put a weight in the center of the line as a tension buffer. A gallon jug full of sea water will work.

SEA ANCHORS

In a heavy sea, the constant jerking of the sea-anchor line can damage a raft, so you should put a weight half way between the raft and the sea anchor to act as a shock absorber.

Some sea anchors have a trip line. Depending on the particular design, this lets you collapse the sea anchor or let water flow unimpeded through it, so you can pull it aboard or vary your speed of drift without the arduous task of pulling it in by hand. (This line may be only 15 feet long, in which case you will have to tie the heaving line to it to lengthen it.) Trip the anchor when you want to drift faster to reach rain, or leave it full during bad weather or when crossing a shipping route.

If your sea anchor does not have a trip line, you can add one yourself. To reduce the chance of fouling the shrouds, the trip line should be polypropylene, so it floats. Attach it to the outside edge of the sea anchor or to where it comes to a point. Make sure it is long enough to let the anchor open full. Leave a slight bow in it, so it doesn't tangle the shrouds. Pull the trip line only far enough to collapse the anchor, not far enough to put a bow in the sea-anchor rode. You don't want to risk tangling. If you have only a nylon line, which will sink, attach a small float 30 or 40 feet ahead of the sea anchor.

Check all the knots and lines from time to time.

SMALL RIGID CRAFT

A rigid craft—such as a dinghy—will be more stable and less likely to ship water if you sit on the bottom rather than on the seats.

Attach the sea anchor to the bow. If you don't have one, try to make one, out of crossed boards, a bucket, a spar, a hatch cover, bleach bottles full of water, anything that will drag through the water.

A float will help prevent a trip line from fouling the sea anchor's rode.

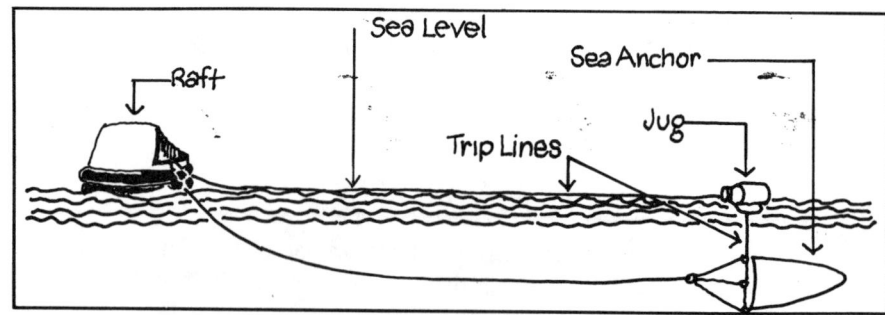

NAVIGATION

A liferaft is no place to learn to navigate, and I don't intend to teach you a full course in it. However, even if you are an experienced navigator, you probably don't use most of what you have learned. As a consequence, you have no doubt forgotten many details and will need to be reminded. I've never met a working navigator who remembered how to figure out a great circle course from tables for more than a week after leaving the Coast Guard testing room. There's no need to.

Someone else might like to learn navigation to pass the time in the raft. Teaching them will give you something to do while it refreshes your memory. I've included more navigation techniques than you are likely to find necessary.

This chapter will explain how much navigation can be done in a liferaft and provide necessary calculator formulas and tables. Formulas are given with the explanations in the main text. Formulas are repeated in the appendix. Tables and a long-term almanac are also in the appendix. All are abbreviated because of space and because there is a limit to how accurate liferaft navigation can or needs to be.

This chapter will also describe primitive substitutes for navigational techniques and instruments that can be made with things that might be at hand on a liferaft. Making a sail is discussed in the preceding chapter.

WHETHER TO LEAVE THE SCENE

This is one of the hardest questions to answer. It depends on a number of things.

Did you get out a distress signal? If so, rescuers will start looking at the position you gave, and you don't want to complicate things by expanding the search area. How accurate was the position?

If you have an EPIRB, they will home on its signal regardless of where you are.

What's the likelihood that anyone heard you? How soon will you be missed? How far is it to land or to a shipping lane? Will wind and current help or hinder you? How much food, water, and gear do you have? How much propulsive and steering control do you have?

Has the abandoned vessel sunk yet? If not, it may be easier to see than a liferaft, both visually and on radar, and you might be able to get back aboard to salvage some equipment or stores. Even if it has sunk, it is wise to wait a while before leaving the area in case something useful floats up. But don't stay directly above it in case the useful something floats up right underneath you.

Discuss your decision with the crew. It is an important one and you don't want to lose their confidence. Tell them what the situation is and why you have decided as you have.

WHERE TO HEAD FOR

You need to find one of three things: rescue, land, or rain.

Finding Rescue

Rescue is most likely in a shipping lane or where fishing boats frequent. The chart on page 175 shows major shipping routes.

Finding Land

In general, unless you are very confident in your navigation and steering skills, head for a place that is big enough to hit. Islands in the ocean are tiny targets at the best of times.

In the open ocean and lacking a better idea, your first direction should be approximately east or west, since most large land masses are oriented more or less north and south, except in the central Indian Ocean.

If the place you're aiming for is so large you can't miss it, such as a continent, steer straight for it. You can always hitch hike home if you're off by a few miles.

If you need to steer for a relatively small piece of land, the safest way to find it is by parallel sailing. Head for a point at the same latitude as the land but far enough east or west of it that when you get to that latitude you will know which direction to turn. This does not require you to keep accurate track of longitude.

The shortest way may not be the quickest. Unless you're in a power-driven lifeboat with plenty of fuel, finding favorable winds and currents are probably more important than going exactly in the direction you'd like. The charts on pages 176 and 177 show typical currents for winter and summer in various seas.

Finding Rain

Unless you have a better idea, downwind is usually toward rain in the open ocean, because the longer wind travels over water the more vapor it picks up.

Rain is common during most of the year in the doldrums, especially on the same side of the equator as the declination of the sun, which is the hemisphere that is having summer. The strip of rain will probably be about 10 degrees of latitude wide. You will seldom find rain in the doldrums south of the equator in the Atlantic or eastern Pacific. You probably won't find it in the Indian Ocean during the months which are summer in the northern hemisphere. In December, the rain is deflected southward near northern Australia.

Dry Trade Winds

The tradewinds are mostly dry, but they blow toward rain. They are found between the doldrums and 30° north or 30° south. They blow from the north-east in the northern hemisphere and from the south-east in the southern hemisphere.

Except during monsoons, the trade winds are typically warm and dry. You will see clouds, and some rain might fall occasionally, but you won't be able to count on enough to survive. The eastern shores of the oceans get the least rain in the trade-wind belts. If you're offshore of a desert, don't count on any rain at all.

In these areas you will have to expend more effort on making a sail and on improving the rain-catching ability of your raft, such as by fashioning sheet-plastic into a catchment. The trade winds blow obliquely toward the doldrums, so do what you can to increase the angle. If you cannot do that, at least get some sail up to increase your speed.

The areas between latitudes 30 and 40, more or less, are zones of high pressure in the summer. Any rainfall at all is an unlikely bonus. In the winter, storms are much more likely, and rain is common.

In latitudes 40 to 60, the temperate zones, you will probably get enough rain to survive on, except that there are fewer fronts and less rain during spring on the eastern shores of the oceans and during summer anti-cyclones.

Rain lessens as you go north from the temperate zone into the subarctic and arctic, but you're more likely to find ice.

Monsoons

During the southern winter, from about May until about September, you will find more rain in the northern Indian Ocean than you ever thought could fall. The wind blows from the south-west, and rain is heaviest near the coasts of India. Lighter (but sufficient) rains fall on Asian coasts east of India.

During the rest of the year, the wind blows from the opposite direction. This wind is hot, dry, and weak. Rain is very unlikely until the wind has blown across the ocean for several hundred miles, and even then it is likely to be sparse and occasional.

In the far western Pacific, the north-east monsoon brings rain from China to Australia from November to March.

During monsoons, the lee sides of islands and larger land masses get much less rain than the weather sides.

Frequent heavy rainfall is common from November to March off the south-east coast of the United States and in the north Caribbean Sea.

Winds blowing offshore from continents seldom bring rain. This is particularly important (and depressing) off the coasts of Chile, California, the Arabian peninsula, north-west Australia, the Mediterranean in summertime, and the west–facing coasts of Africa and of India and Burma during the north-east monsoon.

Hurricanes and Typhoons

Cyclonic storms occur everywhere but in the South Atlantic. They typically start just above or below the doldrums and head west, often curving toward the pole. If you face into the wind from a cyclonic storm in the northern hemisphere, the storm center is 90°-110° to your right. Sometimes this is taught as "to your right and behind you." In the southern hemisphere, it is 90°-110° to your left.

July to October is the typhoon season in the western Pacific. Storms frequently go northward up the China coast, bringing rain as well as high winds.

The hurricane season in the North Atlantic and Caribbean is about the same, sometimes starting earlier and ending later.

DEAD RECKONING

In order to determine where you are by dead reckoning, you must know where you started, how fast you have been moving, for how long, and in what direction.

Knowing where you started requires conscientious navigation before you have to abandon ship. You should salvage the log and maintain it. Once in the liferaft, you should keep a navigation log.

If you determine your position at dawn, dusk, or both, you will not need a watch to estimate time between positions. If you do both, you can assume 12 hour days. The error during daylight will correct for the opposite error at night.

Speed of Travel

Your speed consists of two parts: the speed of the water current and your speed through the water. Set and drift are all you have in a liferaft.

Speed of current can be guessed or determined by consecutive celestial fixes. You might expect 20 to 50 miles a day from some currents, but only 6 to 12 miles a day near the equator. Since you will be going more or less in the direction of the current, you can get by simply by adding the estimated current speed to the speed through the water. As a last resort, you can estimate that the speed of the current is 2% of the windspeed.

You can often tell when you enter an ocean current by a change in the water color or temperature, but not by the fish that stay with you. They will cross the temperature boundary to stay with their 'kelp patty.'

Speed through the Water

Figure your speed through the water at least once a day. If the wind changes, recalculate.

The best way to determine your speed through the water is by using a chip log. To make a chip log, tie your heaving line or heaviest fishing line to some heavy, floating object, such as a jug two-thirds full of water. It should be heavy enough not to be affected by the wind after you throw it in the water but light enough that you can pull it back in. If you have an empty jug, use sea water. It would be a shame if your line broke and you lost some fresh water.

Tie two knots in the line. One should be close to the weight but far enough from it that the weight has settled in the water before the knot goes overboard. The second knot can be at any convenient measured distance from the first.

Set the weight overboard and let the line run freely through your fingers. Measure the time between knots and apply the following formula:

$$\text{Speed} = \frac{.6 \times \text{feet between marks}}{\text{seconds of time between knots}}$$

If you tie the knots 16⅔ feet apart, the formula becomes:

$$\text{Speed in knots} = \frac{10}{\text{seconds of time between knots}}$$

One nautical mile per hour = 1⅔ feet per second.

Pendulums

If you don't have a watch to time the chip log, you can measure it with a pendulum. Just tie a small weight on the end of a string and swing it back and forth. You'll find that it has a natural speed at which it 'wants' to swing.

The period of a pendulum—how long it takes to swing back *and* forth once—depends only on its length. A pendulum with a one-second natural period is 9.8 inches long, from your fingers to the center of gravity of the weight. A two-second pendulum is 39.1 inches long.

Get it swinging until you have a smooth rhythm, and then drop the chip log overboard.

Sea Anchor

Some sea anchors have a trip line, to spill water from the sea anchor. If yours does not, see page 89 for how to rig one.

The wind is likely to be pushing you more or less all the time. If it is pushing you in a direction you want to go, you can trip the sea anchor or the forward ballast pockets to make better time. If you are crossing a shipping lane, you will want to leave them all full, to stay in the lane as long as possible. The makers of Elliot liferafts say that their rafts will sail at one knot over water speed in 20-knot winds without a sea anchor. With a sea anchor out, they will sail at one knot in 40-knot winds.

You shouldn't trip the sea anchor if the weather is very rough, because you might capsize and because you don't want anyone to get seasick. Besides being unpleasant for everyone, seasickness dehydrates the victim.

For the same reasons, don't trip the aft ballast pockets unless the weather is very calm.

If you don't have a line to use to trip the sea anchor, you can haul the anchor in when you want to increase speed. This can be arduous, especially since you're probably weakened. If you do this, keep the anchor ready for streaming if the weather picks up.

Direction of Travel

The easiest way to find your direction of travel is to trail the heaving line behind you and sight along it with a compass to find the reciprocal of your course. Under some circumstances a cross current may introduce an error here, but mostly you will be moving close to the same direction as the wind, and the wind usually goes roughly the same direction as the current.

In the northern hemisphere the current sometimes sets as much as 30° to the right of the wind direction, because current is affected more by the Coriolis effect than wind is. In the southern hemisphere, the current typically sets to the left of the wind.

Compass

Your compass reading will have to be adjusted for variation, but don't worry about a compass error smaller than about 5°. You can't sail a raft that accurately, and you probably can't read a compass within 5° on a tossing liferaft. The isogonic chart on page 178 will give you the variation close enough for lifeboats.

Deviation is probably irrelevant in a liferaft, because there isn't much metal in a raft. Just make sure you don't use the compass while your knife is next to it, and don't store it right over the CO_2 canister.

You can check your total compass error (variation plus deviation) by one of the celestial methods for finding direction. These methods can also be used to determine direction without a compass and without previous knowledge of celestial navigation. Everything is explained in the celestial section of this chapter, starting on page 103.

Figuring Position from Distance and Direction Travelled

There are three ways to find your new position after you know how far you have gone, and in what direction. You can plot it on a chart or plotting sheet, use a simplified traverse table (see page 100), or work it out on a calculator (see page 102).

Constructing a Plotting Sheet

This is pretty easy. You can use either a sheet of paper with a compass rose marked on it or your biggest sheet of blank paper and a protractor.

To make a plotting sheet measuring two degrees by two degrees, you need a circle, a vertical line and a horizontal line crossing at the center of the circle, and two more horizontal lines at the top and bottom of the circle.

The vertical line is your central line of longitude, and the horizontals are even degrees of latitude.

If you are using a radar-plotting sheet, draw the top and bottom horizontals so they touch the biggest circles. If you are using regular plotting sheets or large blank paper, draw the cross first, then center the circle on it. If you don't have better tools, you can make the circle by using a string tied to your pencil. The circle should be 12 inches in diameter. Then draw the other 2 horizontals.

If you are using 8½ x 11 inch paper, make the circle six inches in diameter. This will simplify dividing the longitude later.

To make a plotting sheet measuring one degree by one degree, draw the vertical line near the left edge of the paper and draw two horizontal lines six inches or twelve inches apart. Then draw a quarter circle six or twelve inches in radius, with the center of the circle at the bottom left for the northern hemisphere or at the top left for the southern hemisphere.

Now draw a diagonal line through the center of the circle to the degree mark on the circle that is the same as the latitude you want for the center of the plotting sheet. Measure from the equator northward or southward. The example is for 23° north.

Now draw a vertical line through the place where the diagonal line crosses the circle. This is your second line of longitude. Do the same thing on the left side of the paper for the third line of longitude.

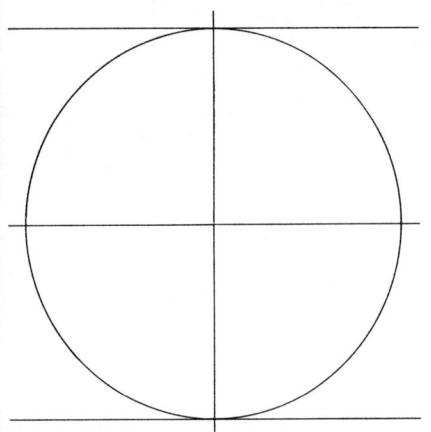

A plotting sheet measuring 2° by 2°.

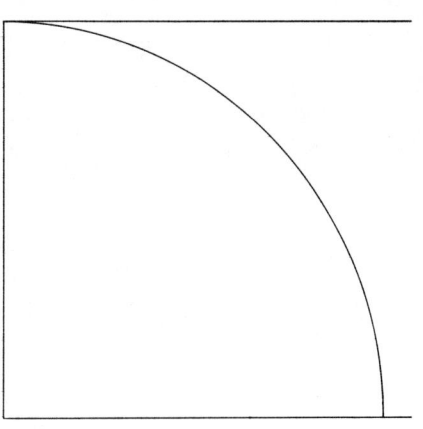

A plotting sheet measuring 1° by 1°.

Drawing the diagonal.

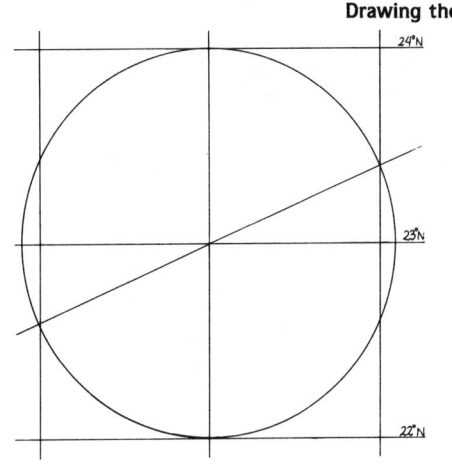

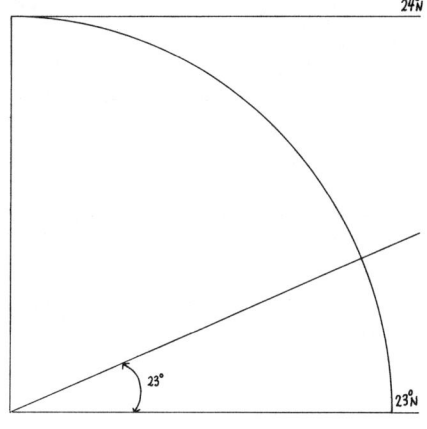

Drawing the vertical.

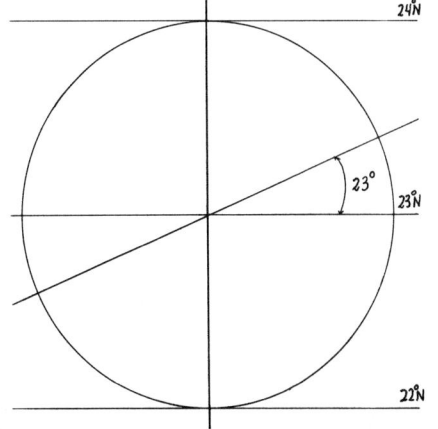

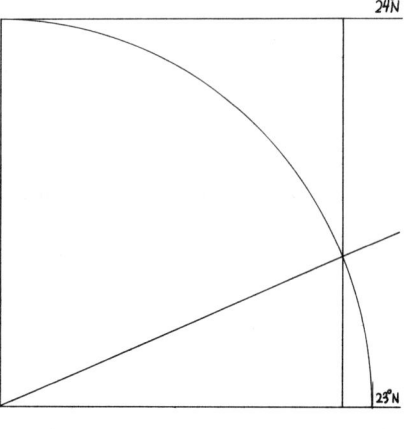

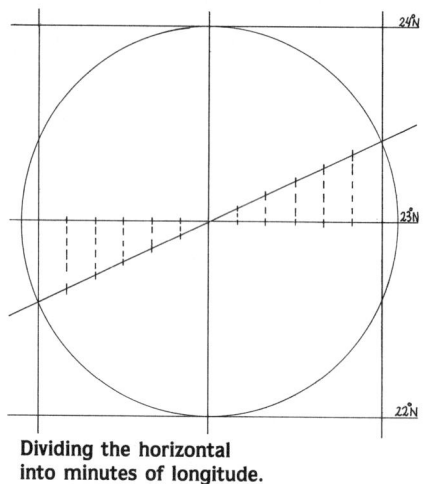

**Dividing the horizontal
into minutes of longitude.**

Divide the vertical lines into minutes of latitude. If the circle has a six-inch diameter, each half-inch represents ten minutes of latitude. If it has a six-inch radius, each inch is ten minutes.

Divide the horizontal lines into minutes of longitude. If you have used a six-inch radius circle, you can easily do this by measuring the inches on the diagonal line and drawing vertical lines through each of the inch marks. These will intersect the horizontal line at each ten minutes of longitude.

New Latitude and Longitude

Once you have determined your distance and direction of travel by dead reckoning, you can get your new lat/lon from a traverse table, with a calculator, or with a pencil and paper.

Traverse Table

This is a simplified traverse table taken from volume 1 of Bowditch.

Table 1
Simplified Traverse Table

Course Angle	0°	18°	31°	41°	49°	56°	63°	75°	81°	87°	90°
Factor	1.0	0.9	0.8	0.7	0.6	0.5	0.4	0.3	0.2	0.0	

Change in Latitude by Traverse Table

To find your change in latitude, enter the table with your course angle. This is not the same as your course. It is the angle of your course measured from north or south toward the east or west. For example, a course of 280° or 080° is a course angle of 080°. (Bowditch would write it N80W or N80E). A course of 190° or 170° is a course angle of 010° (S10W or S10E).

Multiply your distance run (in miles) by the factor below your course angle in the traverse table. Don't worry about interpolating. The answer is your change in latitude, expressed in minutes.

For example, if you started at latitude 30° north, longitude 150° west and drifted 35 miles on course 295°, your course angle is 65° from north to west (N65W). This is between 63° and 69° on the table, and the number below this is 0.4, so you multiply 35 miles times 0.4, which means you have changed 14 minutes in latitude.

Change in Longitude by Traverse Table

To find your change in longitude, subtract your course angle from 90°, and use that to enter the table. Multiply the factor by distance run. This gives you your departure. Enter the table again with the midlatitude, that is, latitude between your start and finish. Divide your departure by the factor below your latitude. This gives you the change in longitude.

In this example, 90° minus 65° is 25°, so you enter the table with 25°. This is between 18 and 31, so the factor is 0.9. Multiply 0.9 times 35 miles run, which gives you a departure of 31.5. Your midlatitude is halfway between 30° north and 30° 14' north. The factor for this is 0.8, so divide the departure of 31.5 by 0.8, which gives you a change in longitude of 39.4 minutes.

If you started at 30° north, 150° west and drifted 35 miles on course 280°, you ended up at 30° 14' north, 150° 39' west.

Sailings by Formula

To figure out your dead reckoning position from a formula involving your course and distance travelled, you must either have a calculator with trigonometric functions built in (most do) or be able to use trig tables, which you probably had to do to get your license. If you have no calculator, you can do it with pencil and paper. Round everything off to make it easier.

Abbreviated trig tables start on page 166. The full table takes up 44 pages in Bowditch. Entries are for every half degree, in decimals. They are accurate within half a degree on bearing problems. If for some reason you need greater accuracy (or just to pass the time), you can interpolate. In most cases you can round the tables more than I did and still be close enough.

Remember, everything must be entered into the calculator as decimals. Degrees and minutes must be entered as decimal degrees. Minutes and seconds must be entered as decimal minutes.

Change in Latitude by Formula:

Your change in latitude equals the distance traveled times the cosine of the course angle.

Distance is entered in nautical miles.

Course angle is not your true course but the angle of your course east or west from north or south. If your course is 295°, your course angle is 65° from north to west (N65W).

Using the same example as with the traverse table, you have drifted 35 miles from position 30° north, 150° west. The cosine of 65° is 0.4226. Round this to .42. You don't need better accuracy on this problem. Multiply 0.42 times 35 and get 14.7 minutes of latitude. Call it 15. In fact, if you really don't like arithmetic, or if you have to do this in your head, you can round the tangent to .4, which yields 14 minutes change in latitude, which is close enough.

Change in Longitude by Formula:

Your change in longitude equals the tangent of the course angle times the change in latitude times the factor in Table 2.

Table 2

Latitude	0°	18°	29°	36°	41°	46°	49°	52°	54°	56°	58°	60°
Factor	1.0	1.1	1.2	1.3	1.4	1.5	1.6	1.7	1.8	1.9	2.0	

Change Long. = (tan Course Angle * Change Lat. * Table 2 factor)

Using the same example as before, the tangent of 65° is 2.1445. Round this to 2.1, or even to 2. Multiply 2.1 x 15 and get 31.5. In table 2 the factor below latitude 29° and 36° is 1.2. Multiply 31.5 x 1.2 and get 37.8, which is your change in longitude, in minutes. Call it 38.

So you left 30°N, 150°W and went 35 miles on course 295° and arrived at 30°15'N, 150°38'W.

You'll notice that this is a mile off from the answer you got from the traverse table. The traverse table is even more simplified. The calculator is more accurate. But it doesn't matter. You can't know your true course or speed close enough to make any difference.

CELESTIAL NAVIGATION

If you have a sextant, a watch, and a calculator you can find your position using the tables in this book. If you don't have a sextant, you can make something that will work well enough. If you don't have a calculator, you can still find your latitude. If you have a watch, you can make a guess at your longitude. If you don't have any tools at all, you can still use the stars to find true north or south or to find your compass error.

In using a calculator, remember that everything must be entered as decimals rather than degrees-minutes-seconds.

After the section on finding GHA and LHA, techniques are divided into finding direction and finding position. Within those categories, procedures are listed more or less from easiest to hardest.

GHA, SHA and LHA

Except for the first few procedures, most of the techniques that follow require you to find either the Greenwich Hour Angle (GHA) or the Local Hour Angle (LHA) of the sun or a star.

GHA is the degrees of longitude that the sun or star is west of Greenwich (technically, the angular distance of the geophysical point). SHA (Sidereal Hour Angle) is the degrees of longitude that a star is west of the GHA of Aries. LHA is the degrees of longitude that the sun or star is west of your position.

GHA of the sun can be found in the long-term almanac in the appendix. (Note that the entries are for every third day, but the gap is four days at the end of the 31-day months and zero days or one day at the end of February.)

To find the GHA of a star, first find the GHA of the first point of Aries on page 156. Figures are given for 0000 hours on the first day of each month. Interpolation instructions are with the almanac. The multiplication table on page 159 will simplify multiplying degrees. For years later than 1989, remember to add the annual correction.

Next find the Sidereal Hour Angle (SHA) of the star. This is the degrees of longitude that the star is west of the GHA of Aries. Find the

SHA in the table on page 157. The table is correct for 1989. Add the annual correction for later years.

GHA star = GHA Aries + SHA star. This is always plus.

LHA = GHA + your longitude if your longitude is east
LHA = GHA − your longitude if your longitude is west

FINDING DIRECTIONS BY THE
SUN AND STARS

Polaris

Polaris is visible from about 5° north latitude and is useful up to about 60°. It is always within 2° of true north, which is close enough for compasses. South of 50°N, Polaris is always within 1° of true north.

When the trailing star of Cassiopeia or the Big Dipper is straight up from Polaris, Polaris is due north of you. When Cassiopeia is to the right of Polaris, Polaris bears 001° (or 002° if you're north of 50°N). When Cassiopeia is to the left of Polaris, Polaris bears 359° (or 358° if you're north of 50°N). See star charts, pages 171 to 174.

South Celestial Pole

There is no noticeable star at the actual south celestial pole. To find the pole, first locate the Southern Cross, which looks like an irregular trapezoid. (See star charts, pages 171 to 174.)

If the Southern Cross is at zenith (which you can determine with a watch and the tables in the appendix), it is directly south from you.

If it is not at zenith, imagine a line through the long axis of the Southern Cross intersecting a line from the northermost star in Triangulum Australe (Southern Triangle). This second line is perpendicular to the line joining the other two stars in the triangle.

Bearing at Rising and Setting

If you're not travelling too fast north or south, which is pretty unlikely in a liferaft, you can determine true north or south by observing the compass direction of any heavenly body when it rises and then when it sets. True north or south is half way between the two. The difference

between this and 000° or 180° on your compass is your compass error.
If a star rises bearing 080° and sets bearing 274°, true south is
$$\frac{80° + 274°}{2} = 177° \text{ on your compass.}$$
Your compass error is 3° E.
You can do this with any celestial body except the moon.

Steering for a Star

If a star or planet has the same declination as the latitude of the place you
want to steer for, then that star is directly over your destination once a
day, when its GHA is the same as the longitude of the destination,
measured westward through 360°.

When the GHA and longitude coincide, the star is exactly in the great
circle direction you want to go, and you can steer for it, to the extent that
you can steer at all. Observe the compass direction.

Meridian Transit

Any celestial body bears due north or south at meridian transit, which is
the time of maximum altitude, when the star crosses your longitude, when
the LHA is zero.

If you have a sextant, take a series of sights to determine when a
body is at its highest (or lowest) altitude. Then find its compass direction.
The difference between it and 000° or 180° is your compass error.

If you have a watch and know your approximate longitude, you can
predict the time of meridian transit as accurately as you know your
longitude. Use the almanac and tables in the appendix to find when the
body's GHA is the same as your longitude west of Greenwich. Observe the
compass direction at the time of meridian transit.

Amplitudes

This is the bearing of a body at rising or at setting. You can do it by table
or with a calculator.

Abbreviations: A = Amplitude of the sun or star
                         L = your latitude
                         d = declination of the body; find this in the
                                   almanac, page 151 or 157.

By calculator:

$$A = \sin^{-1}\left(\frac{\sin d}{\cos L}\right)$$

All terms are positive, even if latitude and declination are different names (one north and one south).

The answer this gives you is an amplitude, not yet a bearing. It is the angle of the body north or south from east or west of you.

The amplitude is east when the body is rising

The amplitude is west when the body is setting

The amplitude is north of E or W when the declination is north

The amplitude is south of E or W when the declination is south.

Example: You are somewhere west of Los Angeles, at about 34° north, watching the sun rise on the longest day of the year, June 21. The declination is 23½° north, which you know from the almanac, page 153.

$$A = \sin^{-1}\left(\frac{\sin 23.5}{\cos 34}\right) = 28.7, \text{ which rounds to } 29$$

Declination is north, and the sun was rising, so the amplitude is E29N, which means the bearing is 29° north of east (090° − 029° = 061°).

If the sun were setting, the amplitude would be W29N, which gives a bearing of 270 + 029 = 299.

On the shortest day of the year in the northern hemisphere, when the declination is 23½° south, the amplitude would be the same, about 29°, but it would be 29° south of east (E29S), which is 090° + 029° = 119° from you. At sunset it would be W29S, which is 270° − 029° = 241°.

If you were at 34° south latitude, the answers would be exactly the same.

By table:

This isn't nearly as accurate as doing amplitudes by calculator, but it is close enough for lifeboats.

Table 3
Amplitudes
Declination N or S

		0°	5°	10°	15°	20°	25°	29°
	0°	0	5	10	15	20	25	29
	10°	0	5.1	10.2	15.3	20.3	25.4	29.5
	20°	0	5.3	10.7	15.9	21.4	26.7	31.1
Latitude	30°	0	5.8	11.6	17.4	23.3	29.2	34.1
N or S	40°	0	6.5	13.1	19.8	26.5	33.5	39.5
	45°	0	8.5	14.2	21.5	28.9	36.7	43.3
	50°	0	9.4	15.7	23.8	32.2	41.1	49.0
	55°	0	10.5	17.6	26.8	36.6	47.5	57.7
	60°	0	12.1	20.3	31.2	43.2	57.7	75.8
	62.5°	0	13.1	22.1	34.1	47.8	66.2	----

Enter the table with your latitude north or south and the declination of the body north or south, and interpolate to find the amplitude of the body.

		Declination	
		20°	25°
Latitude	30°	23.3	29.2
	40°	26.5	33.5

By interpolation, the amplitude is about 29°, which is the angle north or south of east or west. This is explained in the example of amplitudes by calculator on page 106.

Azimuths (Bearings)

An azimuth is the bearing to the point on the horizon directly below the body. If you know your position within a fraction of a degree, you can check your compass against the azimuths of various celestial bodies.

An azimuth gives you an absolute direction, so the difference between the observed bearing by compass and a computed bearing will give you the total compass error, including both variation and deviation. If you are just looking for direction, an amplitude is much easier to do. Azimuths are included here because they do give direction, but they are mainly useful as part of finding your latitude and longitude, which is covered later in this chapter.

To find an azimuth, you'll need a watch and either a calculator or pencil, paper, and the tables in the appendix. The tables are condensed, but they're close enough for azimuths. If you need better accuracy, you will have to interpolate.

There are two formulas for finding an azimuth, the time azimuth formula and the altitude azimuth formula.

In both formulas, if the latitude and declination are of contrary name (one north and one south), enter the declination as a negative number. If the LHA is greater than 180, enter it as a negative number. If the answer you get is negative, add 180 to it.

Your answer will be an azimuth angle, up to 180 east or west from north or south. The azimuth angle starts from the north when you are in north latitude and from the south when you are in south latitude. It goes east or west according to which side of your meridian the body is on. Except at meridian transit, you should have no trouble knowing if the body is east or west of you. It is east if it is rising and west if it is setting.

Abbreviations:

Z = Azimuth
L = your latitude
d = declination of the body
LHA = Local Hour Angle
Hc = Computed altitude of the body

Time Azimuth Formula

$$Z = \tan^{-1}\left(\frac{\sin LHA}{(\cos L \tan d) - (\sin L \cos LHA)} \right)$$

Example: 1000 local daylight savings time, 21 June 1989,
DR position Latitude 34N, Longitude 150W.

GMT = 1900
(Remember daylight savings time when you convert to GMT.)
GHA of the body = 104.5 (in decimal degrees)
  (from the almanac) 175° 33' minus (5 hours times 15°)
LHA of the body = 314.5 (in decimal degrees, rounded)
  104.5 GHA - 150 west longitude = -45.5
  -45.5 + 360 = 314.5 (either -45.5 or 314.5 will work.)
d = 23.5 (in decimal degrees, rounded)

$$Z = \tan^{-1}\left(\frac{\sin -314.5}{(\cos 34 \tan 23.5) - (\sin 34 \cos -314.5)} \right) = -87.5$$

-87 is close enough.

Since the answer is negative, add 180 to it = 93.

Your azimuth angle is 93°. This is not always the same as a simple bearing. To translate the azimuth angle into a bearing, you must know if you are in the northern or southern hemisphere and if the star is east or west of you.

You can tell if the star is east or west by looking at the star or by looking at its LHA. If the LHA is between 0° and 180°, the bearing will be to the west of you. If the LHA is between 180° and 360°, the bearing is to the east. In our example, the LHA is 315.55, so it is east.

If you are in the northern hemisphere, you start from north and count 93° east.

If you are in the southern hemisphere, start from straight south and count 93° east.

Altitude Azimuth Formula

To use this method, you must first find the computed altitude (Hc).

$$Hc = \sin^{-1}[(\sin L \sin d) + (\cos L \cos d \cos LHA)]$$

$$Z = \cos^{-1}\left(\frac{\sin d - (\sin L \sin Hc)}{(\cos L \cos Hc)}\right)$$

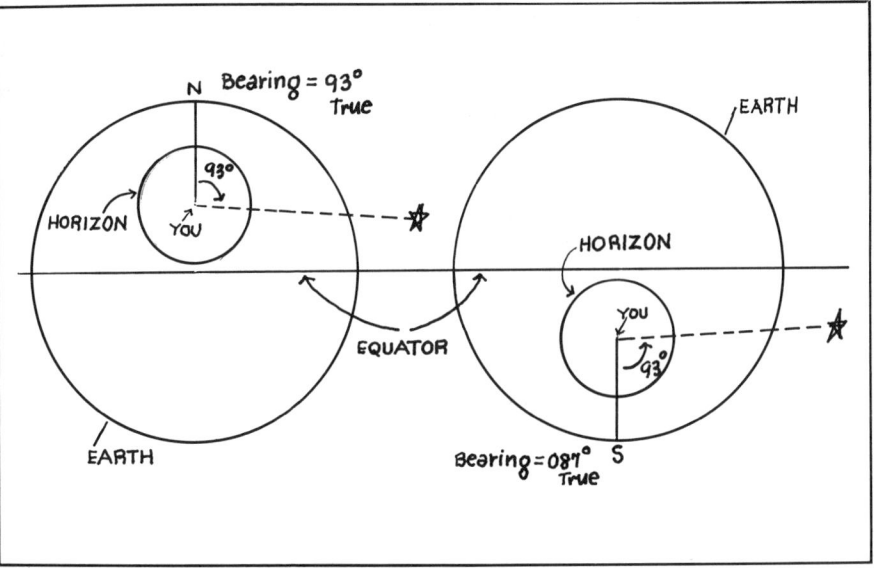

FINDING YOUR LATITUDE AND LONGITUDE

For this, you must either have a sextant or be able to make a substitute. Fortunately, substitutes are easy to make with commonly available materials. It won't be very accurate, but any measurement is better than an estimate.

The easiest and most effective sights will be latitude by Polaris at dawn and dusk or the Sun at meridian transit (local apparent noon).

Try to take your sights from the tops of swells, so you get a better horizon. Take several sights and average them out or pick the one that seems best to you. Try to take sights between 30° and 70° above the horizon. Above or below that, the errors increase dramatically.

If you have a good sextant, you can make the usual corrections, but don't get hung up on it. Don't try to be as good as Loran.

Sextant Substitutes

Astrolabe: Astrolabes were in use long before the sextant. The Arabs invented the astrolabe and made some very fancy ones. Yours won't be so nice, but it will work.

You'll need a flat board, or a compass rose, or both. If you have a radar plotting sheet, tape it to your fish-cleaning board. If you don't have a plotting sheet, use a string and pencil to draw a circle, and then mark off the degrees on it.

There are three ways of using an astrolabe, the shadow method for the sun and two direct sighting methods for stars.

Whichever of these methods you use, it's a good idea to take several sights and average the results. Also, turn the astrolabe upside down and take half the sights that way. This will minimize whatever errors are built into the construction of the astrolabe.

Shadow Method: Put three nails or pegs in the board, one at the center, one on the circle at 90°, and one on the circle at 270°. The center peg must be exactly perpendicular to the board. Hang a weight from the peg at 90°, and tie a loop of string for your finger on the 270° peg. When you hang the astrolabe by the 270° string, the weight at the 90° peg should make the 0°-180° line exactly level.

Hold the astrolabe by the loop of string and turn it so it is on edge to the sun. The shadow of the center peg will fall across the altitude of the sun.

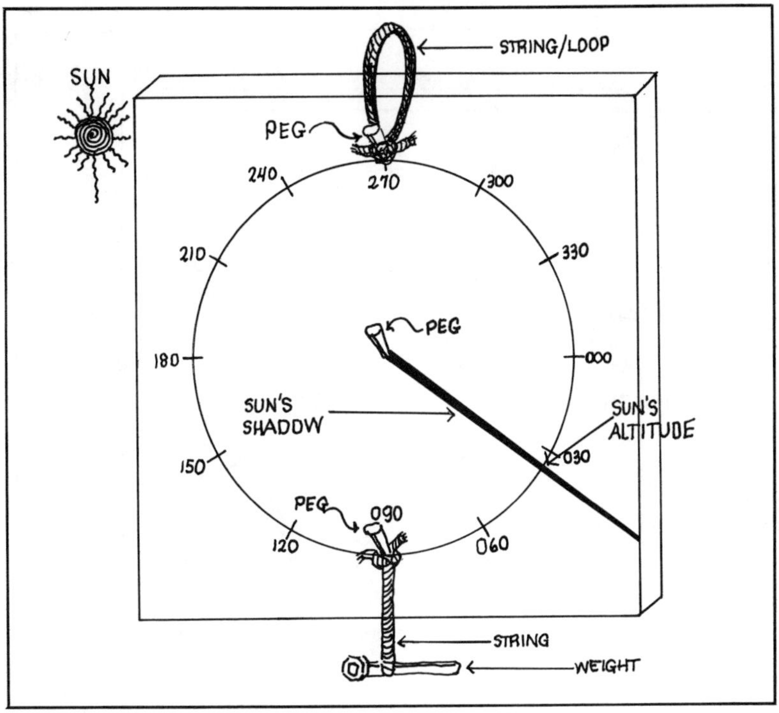

Astrolabe for shadow method of observing the sun.

Astrolabe for direct observer method of sighting stars.

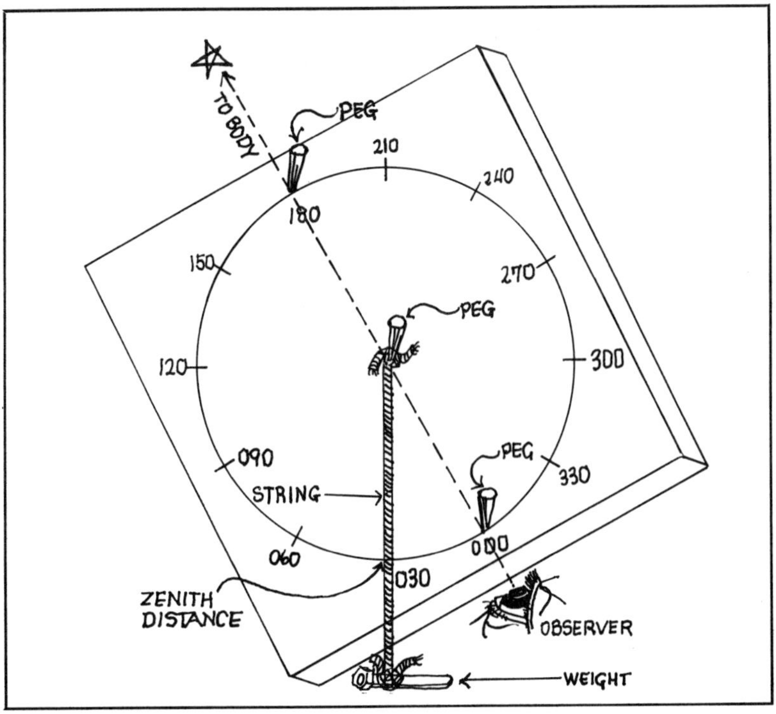

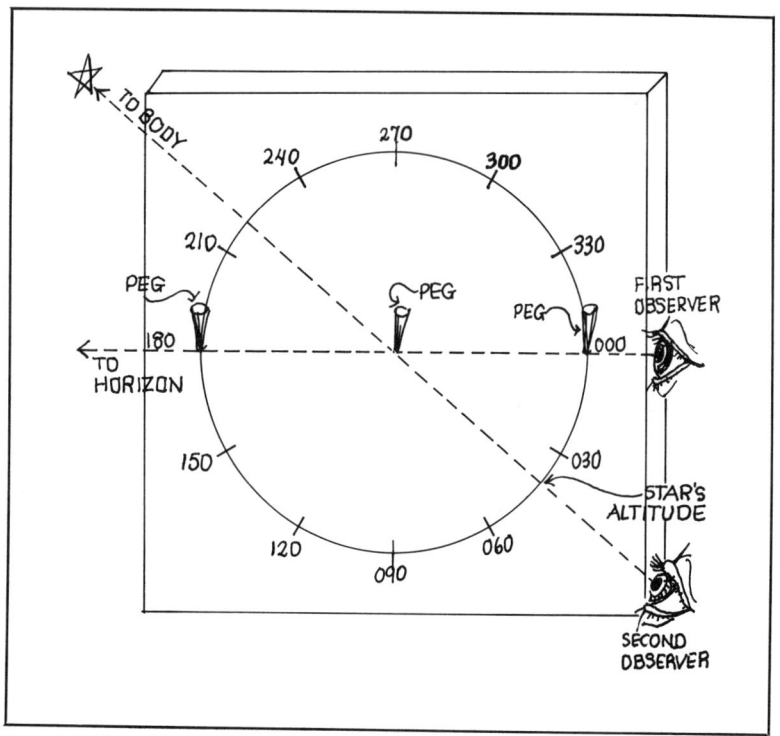

Astrolabe for two observers.

Direct Sighting Method: Put three pegs or nails in the board, but put one in the center and the other two at 000° and 180°. Hang the weight from the center peg.

Hold the astrolabe up and look at the star along the 000°-180° axis. The string holding the weight will hang across the zenith distance of the body you are looking at. Subtract this number from 90 to get the altitude of the body.

Another way is for one person to sight along the 000°-180° pegs to the horizon, while another person looks at the star and finds its altitude.

Cross-staff: A cross-staff is less accurate than an astrolabe and is included only for those who can't make an astrolabe. It is as primitive as you can get and still can be useful for navigation.

To make a cross staff, put two straight pieces of wood together so they make a cross. You can use pencils, but nothing smaller. They must be perpendicular to each other. Raise the device until the horizon appears at the bottom of the short piece. Pull the short piece toward you until the star appears at the top.

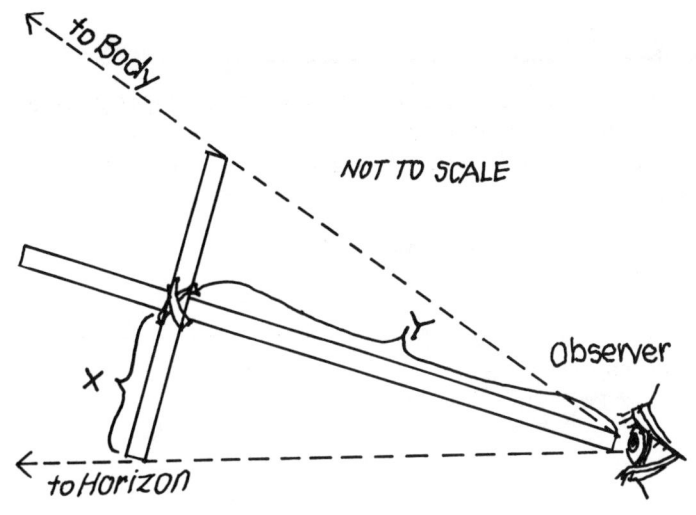

Cross-staff: a makeshift sextant.

Half cross-staff.

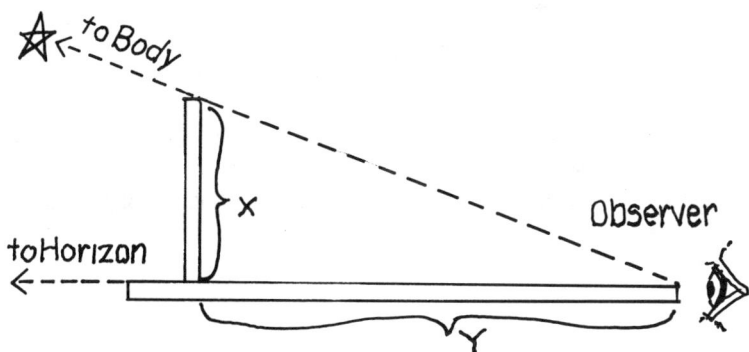

Three sticks and some string: the most primitive possible cross-staff.

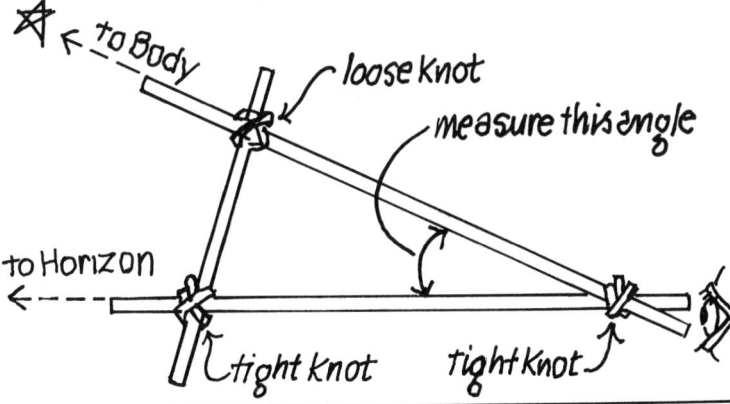

The length of half the short arm (x in the top figure on page 113) divided by the part of the long arm between the short piece and your eye (y) equals the tangent of half the altitude of the star.

$$\text{Altitude} = 2\tan^{-1}\left(\frac{x}{y}\right)$$

Another way to use a cross-staff is to point the long stick at the horizon and sight the star over the cross piece. Or you can make it in a simple L-shape. In this case the formula is

$$\text{Altitude} = \tan^{-1}\left(\frac{x}{y}\right)$$

If you don't have a calculator and can't deal with trig tables, you can still use a cross-staff. After you have taken the sight, measure the angle between the sticks with a protractor.

Protractor and Three Sticks: The last primitive sextant substitute is shown in the bottom figure on page 113. Make a triangle of three sticks. Tie the knot near your eye tight. Of the other two knots, tie one tight and one loose enough to slide. Point one of the sticks at the horizon and another at the sun or a star. Use the third stick to hold on to and to hold the other two in position.

When you have taken the sight, use a protractor to measure the angle between the sticks.

You must realize that there is a limit to how accurate you can be using three pencils and a protractor on a liferaft, and that limit is nowhere near your usual standard, but it doesn't need to be.

Sextant Altitude Corrections

How many corrections you need to make depends on how accurate your sight is. If you have a legitimate sextant, an accurate watch, a calculator or tables, and a stable platform, either because of a calm sea or having washed ashore, you may use them all. If you are using a cross-staff on a raft in 10-foot seas, you can ignore all of them unless you want something to occupy your time. There's little navigational value in making 10 minutes of corrections to a sight that's 2 degrees off. In general, you will do well enough if you subtract 15 minutes for a lower-limb sun sight and do no corrections for a star sight or a middle-of-the-sun sight, such as with the shadow method of using an astrolabe.

Index Correction: This is possible only on a real sextant. Apply it as usual or adjust the sextant.

Refraction: This applies to all observations, and the correction is always minus. If a tenth of a degree is close enough for you, subtract 0.1° for altitudes between 5° and 18°. Don't make any correction for higher altitudes.

If you want better accuracy, use the following table.

Refraction

Altitude	5°	6°	7°	8°	10°	12°	15°	21°	33°	63°	90°
Refraction	9′	8′	7′	6′	5′	4′	3′	2′	1′	0	

The correction for a sighting right on the horizon is 34′; however, sightings of bodies on the horizon are notoriously inaccurate.

Dip: Dip is the error in celestial navigation caused by the fact that the water surface between you and the horizon is curved. It varies with the height of the observer's eye. If you're satisfied with accuracy to a tenth of a degree, ignore dip. If you want to apply it, the dip in minutes is about equal to the square root of the height of the eye in feet. This is always a minus correction.

Semidiameter: This is close enough to 16′ for the sun. The correction is plus for the lower limb and minus for the upper limb.

If you observe the center of the sun, such as with the shadow version of an astrolabe, no correction is necessary.

Parallax: This is useful only for the moon and only if you have a current Nautical Almanac with you. To find the correction, in minutes of arc, multiply 57′ times the factor in the simplified traverse table, page 100.

This correction is always plus.

Bodies on the Horizon: For bodies on the horizon, the sum of the corrections except for height of eye is:

Sun: Lower limb, −18′; Upper limb, −50′.
Moon: Lower limb: +39′; Upper limb, +7′.
Planet or star: −34′.

Sight Reduction

Abbreviations:

Hc = computed altitude; what the observed altitude would be if you were at your assumed (DR) position.

LHA = Local Hour Angle; the angular distance of the body measured west from your assumed longitude.

LHA = GHA + east longitude
or GHA - west longitude

If you're working with stars rather than the sun,

GHA star = GHA Aries + SHA star

L = your assumed latitude.

Z = azimuth angle, which is the bearing of the body measured either clockwise or counterclockwise through 180 degrees, starting at north in the northern hemisphere and starting at south in the southern hemisphere.

If your latitude and the declination of the body are contrary name (one north and one south), make the declination negative.

Computed Altitude Formula:

$$Hc = \sin^{-1}[(\sin L \sin d) + (\cos L \cos d \cos LHA)].$$

Azimuth Angle Formulas: If the LHA is greater than 180, enter the LHA as a negative number. If your answer for Z is negative, add 180 to it.

If you have already found the computed altitude (Hc), you can use this formula to figure the azimuth angle (Z).

$$Z = \cos^{-1}\left(\frac{\sin d - (\sin L \sin Hc)}{\cos L \cos Hc}\right)$$

If you haven't figured the Hc, or if you want to check your answer, you can use the following formula for Z.

$$Z = \tan^{-1}\left(\frac{\sin LHA}{(\cos L \tan d) - (\sin L \cos LHA)}\right)$$

Once you have the azimuth, compare the compass bearing with the computed azimuth. The difference is your compass error.

Determining Position without a Calculator or Tables

If you don't have a calculator and can't do formulas with a pencil and paper, you can't do sight reduction, but you can figure your latitude and longitude separately by several methods.

<u>Latitude by Polaris:</u> This is one of the easiest and most accurate sights. Since Polaris is always more or less exactly at the north celestial pole in the northern hemisphere, the observed altitude of Polaris is more or less equal to your latitude. As stated in the section on finding north, Polaris is visible from about 5° north and is useful up to about 60°. It is always within 2° of true north, which is close enough for compasses but not close enough for latitude, even in a lifeboat. South of 50° north, Polaris is always within 1° of true north, which is better but not as good as you'd like.

When the trailing stars of Cassiopeia and the Big Dipper (see star charts) are east and west of Polaris, the observed altitude of Polaris is exactly the same as your latitude, so you don't have to correct except for the regular sextant corrections.

When Cassiopeia is straight up from Polaris, Polaris is 1° above the celestial pole (or 2° if you're north of 50° latitude). Subtract one degree from the observed altitude to get your latitude.

When the Big Dipper is straight up from Polaris, Polaris is 1° below the pole (or 2° if you're north of 50°). Add 1° to the observed altitude to get your latitude.

If Cassiopeia and the Big Dipper are diagonal, you can guess at the appropriate proportion of 1 degree to add or subtract.

<u>Latitude by Meridian Altitude:</u> This is also an easy and effective sight. It is based on the fact that when a body passes directly north or south of you, the navigational triangle collapses to a line, so it's easier to solve. All you need are tables and a sextant or sextant substitute. The tables are in the appendix.

If you have an accurate watch and some idea of your longitude, you can be ready and take one sight at the right time. Otherwise take a number of sights as the body rises in the sky. When the altitude starts getting lower, stop and use the highest sighting altitude for your figures.

> Your latitude is 90° minus the observed altitude
> plus or minus the declination of the body.

Subtract the declination if the body is north of you in north latitude or south of you in south latitude.

Add the declination if the body is north of you in south latitude or south of you in north latitude.

Unless you are within a degree or two of the equator, the easiest way to know whether to add or subtract the declination is to look at your dead reckoning position and see whether adding or subtracting will get you closest to it.

Longitude by Meridian Transit: You can determine latitude with just a sextant or a sextant substitute, but you need an accurate watch to find longitude.

Take a series of sights of the sun or a star, keeping track of the time you take each one. When the altitude starts going down, stop and use the time of the highest altitude.

Using the tables at the end of this chapter, find the GHA of the body. The GHA of a star is the GHA of Aries plus the SHA of the star.

If you are in west longitude, the GHA of the star equals your longitude. If you are in east longitude, the GHA of the star equals 360 minus your longitude.

RESCUE

SURFACE VESSEL RESCUE

If you are rescued by a surface vessel, it will probably approach so as to put you on its lee side and then drift down on you. Pull in your sea anchor so it cannot foul the rescue vessel's props.

If the rescue vessel intends to tow the raft, attach the tow line to the towing connection, the boarding ladder, or the sea-anchor attachment point. Do not tie it to the life-line.

If the raft is to be hoisted aboard the rescue vessel, hook the line to the towing bridle. Close the aft entryway to keep spare gear from falling out the back.

If the raft must be lifted aboard with injured survivors inside, it must be lifted flat. First inflate the floor hard. Then attach lifting lines to the towing bridles on both sides. Finally, attach two steadying lines to the life-line on each side.

HELICOPTER RESCUE

If you are rescued by helicopter, tie a piece of cloth to an oar and hold it up so the pilot can see the wind direction. Do not fire parachute flares.

The wind from the chopper blades will make balance difficult. Do not stand up unless and until you have to. Everyone should either gather in the center of the raft or spread out evenly. In any case, stay still. When one person is lifted, be ready to rebalance the raft.

When the helicopter drops a sling, it fits around the back and under the armpits. Be careful that it does not tangle or become attached to any part of the raft.

If the helicopter drops a stretcher, detach it from the dropline before you try to put anyone in it.

LANDFALL

HOW TO KNOW IF LAND IS NEAR

The Sky

A single cloud standing stationary in the sky is often directly over land. The same is true of a cloud that remains still while other clouds around it are moving.

Sometimes a shallow lagoon or a sheet of ice will be reflected in the sky. These reflections show up best on the underside of a uniform cloud layer. Both will show up as a light patch in the sky, with the lagoon usually slightly green.

The Sea

Open ocean water is typically darker than coastal water. Really light-colored water indicates shallows. But don't be fooled. Water often changes color at the boundary of the continental shelf, which may be hundreds of miles off the coast.

Waves and swells travel parallel to each other in the open ocean. When they hit an island, it slows down the part that hits it, so the swells bend around the island. On the opposite side, they bend toward each other. An eddy line, a line of turbulence, will extend down swell from the island. If your raft is self-propelled, you can follow the turbulence upswell to land. South Sea islanders traditionally used this technique in navigation. The difficulty is that the eddy-line only shows up down swell, and liferafts are seldom capable of sailing upswell.

The sound of surf, like other sounds, carries well over water, and can sometimes be heard a fair distance from the beach. This may be of help, especially in the fog.

Sometimes you can smell land farther than you can see it. Wood smoke particularly carries well. I used to work with a captain who swore he could smell the western equatorial African coast from 30 miles at sea. I couldn't.

Birds

Land birds get lost, migrate, and are blown out to sea by storms, sometimes hundreds of miles. So don't count on being near land just because you see land birds. Often, you will see sea birds that roost on land, such as frigates or boobies. This too, is not a sign that land is near. Sometimes you will see them hundreds of miles off the coast.

However, sea birds that roost on land typically do so every night, so if they are all going one direction at dawn, they may be coming from land. At dusk, they may all be going toward land. By sea birds that roost on land, I do not mean sea gulls. It is not at all uncommon to see flocks of gulls headed out to sea at sundown. Frigates and boobies are better indicators of relatively nearby land, but they can be misleading, too.

Gulls may fly toward land or toward sea in the evening. Boobies and frigates are more likely to fly toward their roosting place at dusk.

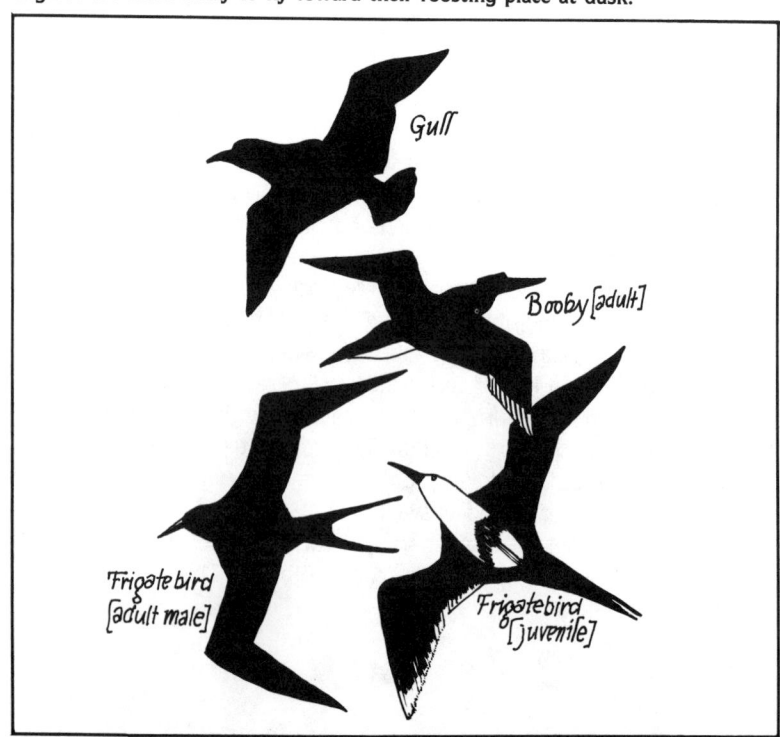

Seals and Sea Lions

Pinnipeds are mostly near-shore creatures. Although I have seen them a hundred miles offshore, their presence is usually a good sign that land is near.

SAILING TOWARD LAND

Winds frequently blow toward land in the daytime and away from land at night. If you see land, you can haul in or trip the sea anchor in the daytime and stream it at night.

MAKING A LANDING

This might be the most dangerous part of your trip, so pay attention and do things right. After spending weeks in a liferaft, it would be a real shame to die in the surf.

Even if you are an experienced small-boat sailor, you must remember that a liferaft is a poor vessel to try to maneuver, and you will not be at your best if you have spent much time in it. Castaways rescued after a few weeks on a raft with limited food and water usually cannot walk at first, even if there is nothing seriously wrong with them. They often have to be carried by their rescuers. So don't think you can body surf ashore. The simplest landing will be dangerous. Be more careful than you would ordinarily think necessary.

If you make landfall at night, it might be wise to wait for dawn before going ashore, so you can see what you must face and what you are doing.

It is difficult to estimate the height of the surf from the sea. It looks smaller than it does from the shore. If you see spray above the surf, it is an indication of hard breaking waves, which usually means high ones.

Some land shapes tend to have higher waves than others. A steep beach on a weather shore will have the worst surf. The lowest surf will be where the waves are bent the most by the shore. A round bay will have lower waves than headlands on either side of it, but the waves will go on for a longer distance, and undertow is more likely. The best place to land will be a bay on the lee side of an island or headland.

If you can avoid it, do not even try to land in the surf, especially on the weather shore of an island. If the land is an island, paddle to the other side. If it's not, paddle or sail along the coast until you find a good place.

If the coast is inhabited, you may be able to attract attention and find out where to land. You can signal with a red flare. If people on shore know international signals, they may respond with landing signals, given later in this chapter.

Going through the Surf

Wear lifejackets, and clothes to protect yourselves from coral and rocks.
Tie everything down. You don't want to lose anything, and you don't want your gear turning into projectiles.

If you have storm oil, this is the time to use it. It will do the most good in the sea anchor.

Leave the sea anchor out. It will help keep you from capsizing in the surf. In a raft, people should stay on the seaward side, to keep the raft from flipping. If you are in a rigid craft with a square stern and absolutely have to go through the surf, stream the sea anchor from the bow and go in stern-first.

If you are in a covered raft, deflate the arches and sit outside the canopy, so you can escape if the raft capsizes. If your raft does not have deflatable arches, cut the canopy and tie it to the arches to get it out of the way.

Depending on the water temperature, fill the raft with water, to make it more stable. Poke holes in the bottom if you have to. But if the water is very cold, the danger from hypothermia may be greater than the danger of capsizing. You will have to decide that at the time. If you do decide to flood the raft in cold water, wait until the last minute to do it.

If you have good control over your sea anchor, you can leave it full-open as waves approach you, to keep you from flipping over, and then trip it after the wave passes, so you slide forward on the back of the wave. If you try this, you must be very quick and pay close attention.

Stay in the raft as long as you can, until you can walk or crawl ashore. If you are dumped out of the raft, hold on to the lifelines, but be careful not to get caught between the raft and a rock or the bottom. If you have to let go, get back to the raft if you can. Swim ashore only if you must.

When you are safely ashore, have the stronger members of your party help the weaker ones. Get everybody out of the water, and then salvage the raft and its contents before it is destroyed in the surf. Remove the CO_2 cartridge so you won't have to sit on it.

SURVIVAL AFTER REACHING LAND

Your immediate needs on land will depend on where you are, how you are, and the time of year. If the weather is cold, fire and shelter will come before water and food, unless you haven't had any water lately. You will die sooner from cold than from thirst.

Fire

To start a fire, first find a spot sheltered from the wind. On an open, windswept beach, you can pile rocks or dig a hole in the sand, piling the sand on the upwind side.

If the ground is covered with snow, build a small platform and heat reflector. If there is snow, there are probably trees. Green logs are best for the platform and reflector. Lay some logs side-by-side in the snow for the platform. Push two sticks into the snow a foot or so apart, angled toward the platform. Lay some logs on it. Tie them if necessary, but the angle should hold them.

Get some dry tinder. Dry grass is good. Pencil-sized dead wood is good; even damp it will burn if it is small enough. You can cut the bark off larger pieces of wood and shave dry wood from the inside. Soft woods make better kindling than hard woods. If there are pine trees around, pitch burns well. So do pine cones. If you have nothing else, use pages from this book, such as the title page or table of contents. Keep your tinder dry in a plastic bag.

Get some bigger wood. Split wood burns better than whole limbs. If it's damp, pile it near the fire to dry.

Pile the tinder into a teepee shape three or four inches high, with the most flammable stuff on the bottom.

There are many ways of starting fires without matches, none of which work very well except in a laboratory. As they say, if you want to start a fire by rubbing two sticks together, make one of them a match.

There are two exceptions to this: signal flares and a bow and string. Flares will burn anything, so be careful. To use a fire-starting bow Boy Scout fashion, cut a stick a couple of feet long and tie string to both ends. Leave enough slack so you can loop it around

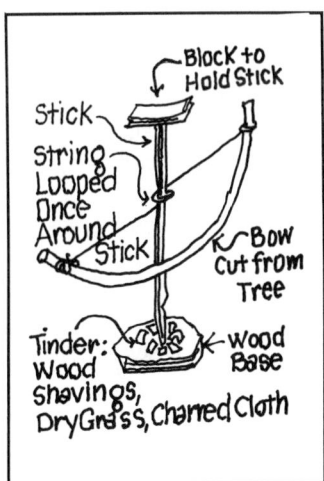

a second stick, the one that will twirl. Gouge holes in two blocks of wood, one to use as a base and one to keep the top of the stick steady. Place some tinder at the base and twirl the stick steadily and quickly.

If you have matches and a candle, use the match to light the candle and then to light the kindling. Protect the match from the wind with your body or cupped hands. Touch the flame to the kindling as low as possible, because flames climb. If the kindling does not light on the first match, use the candle, but hold it as close to vertical as possible, so it won't melt away. You may need it again. Within this constraint, touch the flame to the kindling as low as possible. Let the candle burn until you are sure the fire will not need restarting.

Blow lightly on the fire. This adds oxygen. But don't blow too hard or you'll blow it out.

Add new kindling and then firewood above the flames.

Small fires are better than big ones. They use less fuel. They are easier to control. And you can get closer.

It is easier to keep a fire going than to restart one, so try to make it last overnight. Put two or three chunks of wood on it. When they are well started and you have a good bed of coals, cover the fire with a thin sheet of ashes and then dry earth. It should still be smoldering in the morning.

Shelter

A liferaft with its canopy intact is an excellent shelter, but you may have had to cut the canopy, and it may in any case be too small to lie down in. If so, you will have to build one.

First find a good site. Look for level ground, protected from the wind, with plenty of shelter-making material, water, and firewood available nearby. If you have just spent a month in a liferaft, you will not be able to walk far, but if you have washed ashore after just a couple of days, you can afford to look for a good place. Do not camp under a coconut tree. Coconuts fall.

Put down a ground cloth of sheet plastic. You can use the raft canopy if you're not going to use it for a roof. Or you can use the inner bottom of the raft. The outer bottom probably has barnacles.

If it's cold, stop and rest frequently. Don't work hard enough to sweat. The sweat will evaporate and make you colder.

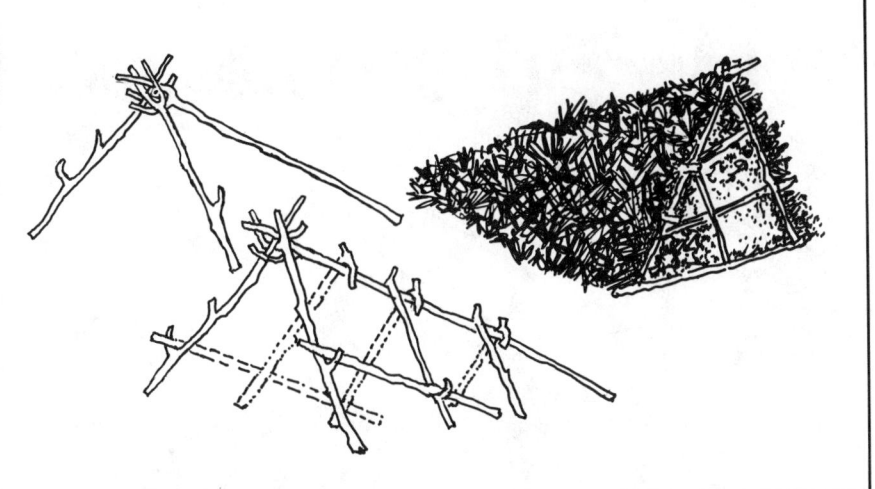

Building an A-frame shelter.

If you have washed ashore where there are trees and branches, the simplest kind of shelter to build is an A-frame. Ideally the ridge pole should be about twelve feet long. The two sticks holding it up should be jammed into the ground six or seven feet apart. A few more sticks for the frame, and then you can cover it. You can use the canopy of the raft or any plastic sheeting. If you don't have enough ready-made material, cut boughs or fronds off trees.

Make a bed of some sort of vegetable material, such as grass, evergreen boughs, or seaweed. If you are cutting branches off trees for this, don't make them too big, because you have to sleep on them.

Snow Caves

If you have come ashore in the snow, you can build a snow cave, which will be warmer than you think. Dig down and then up to keep the heat in. Punch a ventilation hole at the top and keep it open. Pile stuff in the doorway, but don't close it off completely; leave a small opening for air circulation. Build a bed of boughs, leaves, grass, bark, plastic sheeting, bits of canopy, anything to keep you from lying directly on the snow. Snow is a good insulator, so your body heat should be able to make a cave like this pretty snug, but stay bundled up. It is obviously not going to get much warmer than 32 degrees or your shelter will melt around you. A candle can increase the warmth. The main advantage of a cave like this is that it gets you out of the wind.

Dig a snow cave upward to trap the heat, then block the entrance.
Punch a hole in the top for ventilation.

WATER

On low-lying islands you may be able to dig for water. This should be done in a low area inside the vegetation line, not on the beach. (Don't count mangroves as part of the vegetation line, because they grow with their roots in salt water.) Do not dig any deeper than you have to, because the water may get saltier as you go deeper. A foot deeper than the water line should be enough. The freshest water will be on top, so use a bailer or a shell to skim off the good water. If the water is too salty, try another hole.

In the jungle, hanging vines are often filled with liquid. Cut a vine, put one end in your mouth, and notch the vine a few feet higher to let air in and let the water run out.

Solar Stills

On land, solar stills are easier to make and operate than on a bouncing raft. Dig a hole in full sun, three or four feet in diameter and a couple of feet deep. Put a bucket in the center of the bottom of the hole.

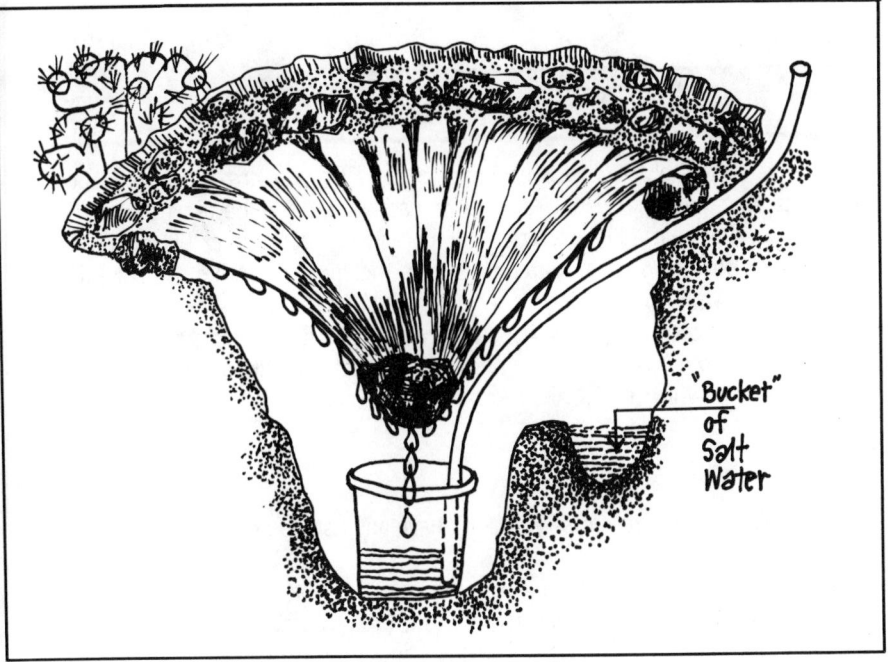

A solar still on land can be dug into the sand or dirt.

If you have some plastic tubing, tie it so you can suck water out without having to take the whole thing apart. It takes 30 minutes to an hour to resaturate the air after you open it up.

Cover the hole with sheet plastic. Put a rock in the middle of the plastic, so it forms an inverted cone directly above the bucket. Put a row of rocks around the hole, anchored with sand and rocks on the top. Make sure the plastic sheeting does not touch the sides.

You can increase the amount of water you get by putting a bucket of salt water in the hole, off to the side. Or you can put vegetation in the hole, especially succulents.

In the arctic you may have to melt ice or snow for water. Ice melts faster than snow and yields more water per cubic inch.

Purifying Water

If you are doubtful about the safety of water you find, you can purify it with iodine from your first-aid kit. Use a couple of drops per quart of water. The Marines mix one canteen capful of iodine with a single canteen of water and then mix one capful of that mixture with another canteen of water to drink. Chlorine bleach can also be used to purify water, but be careful not to use too much.

FOOD

Food is not likely to be a problem onshore if you are willing to eat things that look disgusting and taste bad. Cooked is better than raw, because the heat kills bacteria and parasites, but raw is better than starving. Boiling in fresh water preserves the most nutrients. Be sure to save the water for drinking.

You can also wrap food in seaweed and bake it. Put a *dry* rock in the fire, and lay the wrapped food on it when it's hot. (A wet rock can explode when water which has soaked into cracks expands into steam.)

Sea Animals

Most fish are good to eat. If you don't have any fishing gear, you can make a spear.

Watch out for fish that eat coral; they may be poisonous. You can recognize them by protruding front teeth. (See the sections on poisonous fish, page 44, and fish with poisonous stingers, page 63.)

As a general rule, do not touch any fish that looks like a rock, puffs up, or has protruding teeth. (See the section on fish subject to ciguatera poisoning, page 44.) You can eat these fish if it is absolutely necessary. First, fillet them very thin. Soak the fillets in several changes of water and discard the water. Finally, boil the fish and throw away this water as well.

Most shellfish are good to eat. Big is better than small, but small is more common. Small snails and limpets are found nearly everywhere. Cooked is better than raw, to kill bacteria.

Do not eat shellfish that you find dead or that you find alive among a lot of dead ones. Do not eat mussels, clams, or cockles from April to October in the northern hemisphere. During this time of year they often consume things that make them poisonous.

Do not touch cone shells; they have poisonous stingers (see page 69). In general, do not pick up any pointed, spindle-shaped shells.

Seals are the best source of food in the arctic. In addition, their blubber can be burned as fuel and the skin used for shoes. To catch them, wait by an airhole in the ice, and hit them with a stick when they come up to breathe. Or use your biggest hook and line a few inches below the surface. When one bites, pull it up and whack it in the head.

Turtles lay eggs on tropical sandy shores. You can find them by following turtle tracks from the surf line. They may be buried two feet deep. Boil them.

Land Animals

Snakes and lizards are good to eat. Cut off the heads and gut them. The skin will peel off easily. Then boil or roast.

Small rodents such as mice are good to eat. Cut off the feet and gut and skin them. Pound the remainder (including the head) until the bones are ground up enough to eat. Boil them.

Bigger rodents (rabbits and squirrels) are just as good, but the bones are too big to mash up like mice bones.

Land birds tend to be better to eat than sea birds. If you have a fire, pluck the bird rather than skin it, because the skin has a lot of fat in it.

Capture birds and rodents with snares or deadfalls. You may be able to kill or stun shore birds by throwing a stick or rock into a flock of them. Both methods require practice and luck.

Plants

Seaweeds are edible and full of vitamins and minerals, but they don't have many calories. And they do have salt, so make sure you have enough water.

Pigweed (purslane) is a red-green succulent with yellow flowers. It often grows in patches and stands up to a foot high. It is good to eat and has a lot of moisture in it. Eaten fresh, it tastes like watercress and like sour spinach if you cook it. This and fish will keep you alive indefinitely.

Here are some general rules for adding plants to your diet:

— Roots and tubers are more nutritious than greens.
— You can make a tea of chopped evergreen needles, which have a lot of vitamin C.
— The inner bark of poplars, cottonwoods, willows, birches, and conifers is good to eat and nutritious.
— Cattail pollen is very nutritious and can be baked into a tasteless biscuit. Cattail roots and young shoots are good to eat.
— All grass seeds are edible, but do not eat them if they have turned black.
— Most blue and black berries are edible. Some red berries are edible. Most white berries are poisonous.
— Do not eat anything that looks like a bean, cucumber, melon, or parsnip, or which has foliage that looks like dill, parsley, parsnips, or carrots.

— Do not eat any plant which has orange, yellow, red, dark, or soapy-tasting sap, or sap which turns black after being exposed to air.
— Do not eat any plant which has a milky sap. Exceptions include dandelions, wild figs, and papaya. But be cautious; you had better know what you're eating.
— Do not eat the seeds of fruits.
— Never eat mushrooms you find in the wild. They don't have enough food value to warrant the danger.
— The fact that an animal eats something does not mean it is safe for you. Many animals eat things that are poisonous to people.

SIGNALS

Once you are warm, dry, watered and fed, you will need to attract attention. A radio or an EPIRB is best. If you see an airplane or ship, use the signal mirror. In addition, there are two other ways of signaling from land: smoke and a letter signal.

Smoke and Fire

If you have matches, prepare — but do not light — a big fire. If you have plenty of space and materials, make three of them a hundred feet or so apart. Make sure you won't burn down the forest when you light them.

Ideally, you would like the smoke to contrast with the background. You can make white smoke by adding green leaves, ferns, damp grass, moss, seaweed, or a small amount of water. You can make black smoke by adding bits of your raft.

If you have unlimited materials, light the fire and keep it going until someone sees it. Otherwise prepare it but do not light it until you see a ship or airplane.

Letter Signals

In international codes, V means "I require assistance," and W means "I require medical assistance." An arrow means you are proceeding in that direction. Some land folk use X to mean "I require medical assistance."

You are trying to attract the attention of airplanes, so pick a place that is open to the sky. It is essential that your message does not look like a natural formation. Use a color that contrasts with the ground. In snow, use dark branches. On sand, use dark seaweed. Make the letter big, say 20 feet long or more. Each line in the letter should be about six times as long as it is wide. Make the lines straight and the angles sharp.

If you have nothing but sand, dig a square-bottomed trench. The shadows will be visible from the air. In most latitudes, this means you must orient it east and west, so there will always be a shadow, but if your latitude is the same as the declination of the sun, orient it north and south.

Landing Signals

If you do attract the attention of a ship and they send a boat for you, you will have to tell them where to land. You can do this by waving your arms or a white flag or white light, or by shooting off flares. In general, vertical motions mean affirmative and horizontal motions are negative; green is affirmative, red negative. To indicate that this is the best place to land:

— Wave your arms or a white flag or a white light in a vertical motion.

— Or fire a green flare or parachute flare.

— Or flash K (long-short-long) by signal light.

To indicate this is a bad place to land:

— Wave your arms or a white flag or a white light in a horizontal motion.

— Or fire a red flare or parachute flare.

— Or flash S (short-short-short) by flashing light.

To indicate landing here is bad — over there is good:

— Wave your arms or a white flag or a white light in a horizontal motion. Then put the white flag or white light on the ground and carry another white flag or white light in the direction of the good landing.

— Or fire a red flare or parachute flare straight up and then fire a white parachute flare in the direction of safe landing.

Ship Signals to You

To indicate that you are seen and that help will be sent as soon as possible, the ship should fire an orange smoke signal, or three thunder-light signals at one-minute intervals, or three white parachute flares at one-minute intervals.

THIS IS THE BEST PLACE TO LAND

DAY SIGNALS

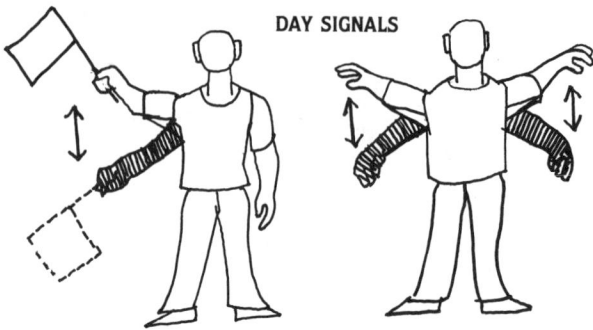

VERTICAL motion of a white flag or of the arms

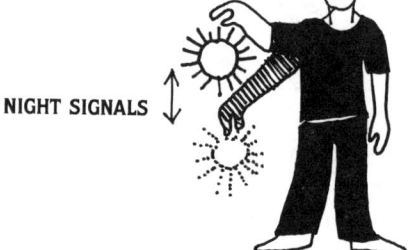

NIGHT SIGNALS

VERTICAL motion of a white light or flare

LANDING HERE HIGHLY DANGEROUS

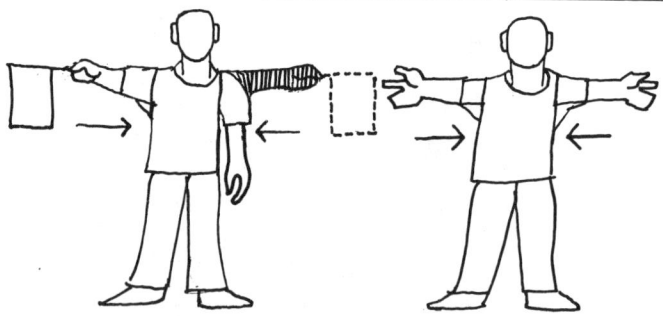

HORIZONTAL motion of a white flag or of the arms extended horizontally

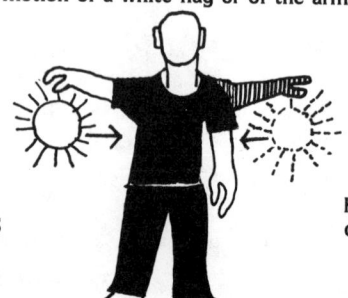

NIGHT SIGNALS

HORIZONTAL motion of a light or flare

MAKING A SURVIVAL KIT

You cannot buy a survival kit as good as you would like. You will have to put it together yourself. Commercially packed rafts include a certain amount of equipment and supplies but not enough. This is not the raft-makers' fault. They know what you will need in order to survive and they give you just enough for a short stay. We know from talking with survivors what they wished they had had, but a full kit is too big and too expensive for most people to think about buying until they are actually adrift in a raft. And it is not economically worthwhile for raft-makers to offer a good kit for sale.

What to include in a survival kit depends on your pocketbook, how much space you have available, where you will be sailing, the size of the ship's company and your personality. Anyone who carries a tool kit in the trunk of the car will want a more extensive ocean survival kit than one who doesn't, and will carry it on shorter trips.

STANDARD ISSUE

The ordinary inflatable liferaft certified for ocean service will include some or all of the following inside the canister. Find out what your raft has in it and, if anything is missing, add it to your own kit. Here is what you can expect to find:

Air Pump: This is usually a foot-pump for pumping up the raft if it loses air. The difficulty is in using it. On land you would put the pump on the ground and step on it. This is impractical on the inflated floor of a rubber raft. You will have to squeeze it in your hands or put it on your fish-cleaning boards.

The pump in the Robertsons' raft never worked. They had to cut off the hose and blow up the raft by mouth once an hour. Dougal Robertson recommends that you carry a mouthpiece to stick onto the hose in case you have to inflate it the hard way. His raft seems to have been a lemon.

Bailer

Can Opener: The bread is usually supplied in cans. (In lifeboats, the water is also stored in cans.)

De-salting Tablets: To make sea water safe to drink.

Drinking Cup: Graduated, for rationing water.

First-aid Kit: Some raft-makers provide kits that are much better than others. Most are minimal, and you can ignore their contents when making up your own first-aid kit. Check your raft's literature to see how much you will need to add. (A full kit is described later in this chapter.)

Fishing Kit: This is often worthless, although it may be enough to get by on. Plan to stock up on tackle.

Flashlight: With spare bulb and batteries.

Hand Flares: You will probably need more.

Heaving Line: This is usually 100 feet of 1/4" polypropylene, to throw to other survivors and pull them to the raft. It should have a rubber donut (quoit or lifesaver) on the end.

Knife: This is round-pointed to prevent poking a hole in the raft. It is intended only for cutting the painter which ties you to the sinking vessel. It won't do for cleaning fish.

Paddles: These are for escaping from a burning or sinking vessel. Do not expect to row to land with them. They will do double duty as shark clubs.

Provisions: This could be a pound of vitamin-fortified bread per person, or it might be limited to some hard candy.

Raft Repair Kit, possibly including clamps or plugs: This may well be hard to use at sea. The patches are applied with a glue that requires a dry surface to adhere to. You had better carry some extra plugs and clamps.

Rocket-propelled Signals: Ships often don't see very well, so you can never have enough of these.

Sea Anchor: Sometimes two.

Seasickness Pills

Signaling Mirror

Sponges: These are for drying the bottom of the raft. This is important to minimize heat loss and to prevent salt-water sores.

Water: Usually a pint for each person the raft is intended for, but it may be as much as six pints per person. It is normally packed in four-ounce plastic pouches, which means four pouches to a pint.

Whistle: This is to let survivors in the water know where the raft is so they can swim to it in the dark or fog. Each lifejacket should also have a whistle attached, so people in the raft can tell where to throw the heaving line, but don't count on it.

THE BARE ESSENTIALS

A Bag to Hold the Kit

I suggest that you assemble the rest of the kit and then see how much space it takes up and how big a bag you will need. The bag should be waterproof and very sturdy. It should be airtight enough to float. The best ones are sold in diving shops, which also sell other things you will want.

Pack everything inside the bag in individual waterproof plastic bags, even things that water cannot hurt. This will help maintain buoyancy if the bag is ripped, and you can use the bags later to store rainwater. Tie several empty, tightly capped bleach bottles to the handles of the bag. This will ensure that the bag will float. Test it to make sure. You will have lots of uses for plastic jugs.

Put this book in the bag, on top, face up, where you can find it easily.

Keep the Kit Handy

Tie your survival kit to the liferaft cradle with a slip knot or other quick-release mechanism. If you ever need it, you may not have time to pull it out of a locker or undo a shackle.

Now, let's consider the items that should be added to your kit. What follows is a list of things you will find useful in the event of a disaster. Some of the equipment is expensive. Most is not. Some items overlap; if you get one, you will not need the other. Some are available in different grades of quality and cost. A few are luxuries.

THINGS TO ATTRACT ATTENTION

Dye Marker: Equip your raft with at least two. If your raft has one, you will use it the first day. If you are adrift long enough to need this book, you will need another marker for when you drift under a flight route.

EPIRB (Emergency Position-Indicating Radio Beacon): This constantly transmits a signal on the distress frequency. Satellites pick up the signal, pinpoint your location, and alert rescuers. This helps most if you are within rescue range of a port, but in any case shipping in the area will be given the location of the distress signal.

The system works. It has aided in 500 sea rescues and 700 land rescues since the first satellite went up. Before then, ships and planes were equipped with receivers, but a ship had to be fairly close, and a plane had to be overhead.

The EPIRB comes with a strong nylon cord coiled around it. Do not tie this cord to the vessel. The device will be worthless if it goes down with the ship.

Flares and Smoke Devices: Pack half a dozen red flares and half a dozen smoke flares. The liferaft will have some as standard equipment, but not enough. You might have to wave your flares at a dozen ships before being seen.

A flare pistol is also a good thing to have, along with a supply of parachute flares.

Radar Reflector: Occasionally a raft will be supplied with one of these. It consists of three aluminum disks, folded flat for storage. In use, they extend outward and form an angular sphere. The disks reflect radar waves directly back to the source. The raft cannot reflect radar waves at all, but a radar reflector will look like a ship on radar. The only difficulty with the reflector is getting it high enough in the air to stand out from the sea clutter.

Signal Mirror: This is usually a round mirror made of metal, about six inches in diameter. It is shiny on both sides and has a hole in the middle.

VHF Radio: Ships do not always watch very well. In mid-ocean, they mostly look out for what they expect to see, other ships, which will show up on radar. Survivor after survivor tells of shooting off flares right in front of ships and watching them pass by. Nine ships passed Steve Callahan.

Ships do usually monitor channel 16 on the VHF, and this is the best way to get their attention. The best hand-held sets receive all channels and cost several hundred dollars. The cheaper ones get fewer channels and still cost a couple of hundred dollars, but they represent the quickest way of being picked up. Everything electronic is getting cheaper. These probably will, too.

Keep the battery charged and carry a spare. Non-rechargeable batteries hold their charge longer than rechargeable ones do. If your vessel has a lifeboat with a battery in it, try to get a radio that uses the same voltage. Carry a two-conductor wire.

You may want to use the radio in ordinary day-to-day operations aboard your vessel and be prepared to grab it in an emergency. If so, it would be wise to store it near whatever navigation tools you intend to take with you in the raft.

THINGS WHICH WILL PROTECT
YOU FROM EXPOSURE

Dry Clothes: If you have room enough and not too many people to keep warm.

Blankets: These take up too much room to put in the bag, but by all means take them if you have time to grab them on the way off the ship.

Space Blankets: These are thin, inexpensive sheets of mylar plastic that allow no body heat to escape because they are so reflective. They are crinkly and a little uncomfortable by themselves, but they keep you warm.

A space blanket on top of a regular blanket is the warmest thing imaginable and is more comfortable.

Try to take one for each person on board. They won't take up much room and they have other uses, too, such as catching rainwater.

The same material is made into a kind of survival suit, which the manufacturer says will extend survival time in the cold by 50 per cent to 70 per cent. They are designed to be worn in the raft not in the water, but they should help there, too, by limiting water circulation around you.

Survival Suit: This is the best protection against cold water. Survival suits are expensive and bulky, but nothing else will do what they do. You can last for hours and hours in water cold enough to kill you in minutes. Naturally, they will keep you warm in the raft, too.

WATER . . . AND HOW TO GET IT

Water: Carry water in pint plastic bottles with screw tops. Start off well stocked and use rain or solar stills or a reverse-osmosis unit to replenish your supply.

Hand-Powered Reverse-Osmosis Watermaker: This is the most important single item you will carry. Exposure and lack of water kill people in liferafts. This device takes care of lack of water. Just drop the hose in the sea (or a bucket of sea-water) and pump. Fresh water comes out the other end. You have to pump it 30 times a minute for maximum output.

The only hand-held model on the market comes in two sizes. The smaller one makes two pints an hour at maximum output. If you pump it 24 hours a day, it will make enough water for eight people to drink as much as they want or enough for 24 people to survive indefinitely. (It will support up to 48 people provided temperatures remain moderate.) It takes up very little room and weighs 2½ pounds.

The bigger one makes 1.4 gallons per hour, enough to give 45 people all they want to drink. It is just a bit larger than the hand-held model and weighs seven pounds.

There is a 12-volt version of the big one, with a manual backup. If you get this one to use as the water supply on a cruising sailboat, make sure you locate it and arrange the connections so you can easily disconnect it if you have to abandon ship.

The manufacturer recommends replacing the seals and o-rings after 600 to 700 hours of operation, which would be 25 to 28 days of straight pumping. An inexpensive kit is available, and it would not hurt to have it along.

Watermakers are expensive. Whether they are worth it depends on your budget, how likely you think it is that you'll spend a long time in a liferaft, and how much you want to survive.

Solar Still: If you spend more than a couple of weeks on a raft without a reverse-osmosis watermaker, this device will save you if anything does. It is available in capacities ranging from two to eight pints per day. Don't expect to get full volume.

The biggest problem with solar stills is that they require full sun and calm water to work. They are also somewhat fragile. Still, I would rather have one than die of thirst.

Some liferafts come with a solar still. If yours does, take a spare. If it doesn't, take two. Better yet, take one for each two people you expect to have on the raft. Not only will you be better off with more stills operating, but when they break, you will be able to cannibalize one for parts to fix another.

De-salting Tablets: These make the water look bad and smell bad, but you can drink it. Drop one tablet in a pint of sea water. If you have a reverse-osmosis unit, you will not need these or stills. If you have solar stills, take some pills along for when the stills break or for bad weather. The water cleaned by one tablet per person per day is the minimum long-term survival ration.

Sheet Plastic and Surgical Tubing: This is intended mainly to catch rainwater, but in a pinch it can be used to make a solar still. Get clear plastic, at least six feet square, and a minimum of six feet of surgical tubing.

The tubing will run from the plastic outside to your water jugs inside. In a solar still, it will run from the fresh-water cup outside, so you will not have to dismantle the still to take a drink.

Solar Shower: A solar shower is a water bag made of clear plastic on one side and black plastic on the other. It has a handle on one end and a hose with a nozzle on its end coming out of the other end. They typically hold two gallons of water. When the sun hits the clear side, it heats the water. This is a luxury. It can be justified simply as a water container, but it has three other possible uses:

1) In cold seas, a cup of hot water will be a treat and possibly therapeutic, especially if you pack some instant coffee or tea or bouillon as well.

2) The venom from many sea creatures can be broken down by heat, and this is likely to be your only source of heat.

3) If you reach a point where the only water you have left is too disgusting to drink, you can absorb up to a pint a day (enough to keep you alive) by enema. One castaway who knew about this had no means of giving himself one. The solar shower bag is ideal for this purpose. The nozzle isn't perfect, but it will work. It will work better if you cut the fat end off the nozzle. This will not be your first choice of a way to get water into your system, but it is a way, and if it comes down to it you'll be happy for it.

FOOD

Freeze-dried Food: This is a great invention. It takes up very little room and tastes good. But you have to have water to eat it. If you have a reverse-osmosis watermaker, use all the extra room in your bag for food. (You will still need to pack *some* plastic bottles full of water.) Concentrate on starches. The fish you will catch are all protein and fat.

If you do not have a watermaker or solar still, take hard candy instead of dehydrated food.

Vitamins: Fish provide calories, protein, and fat, but vitamins are usually found in vegetables, which are rare on liferafts. Make sure the tablets include iron, to avoid anemia.

Plankton Net: This is a fine-mesh net a foot or so across the throat. Tow it behind the raft to gather plankton, which are tiny sea creatures that float rather than swim. They form a gooey mess which tastes something like pablum, but they are extremely nourishing.

FISHING GEAR

This is a place to splurge, because fishing gear is cheap, and it doesn't take up much room.

Hooks: Get 10 each or more loose and 6 each or more with wire leaders. You will need several sizes:

#8 for triggerfish and other scavengers
#4 for the same scavengers
#2 for skittish dorado
#1/0 for hungry dorado.

Buy a few large, barbed hooks with long shanks to make and repair a gaff.
    If you really want to try to catch a shark, which I do not by any means recommend, get some big hooks, at least 10/0, and some heavy wire and heavy swivels. One or more empty bleach jugs will make it easier. Wire the hook to the bottle so the shark cannot dive. It kills itself trying.

Line: You will have use for a spool of each of several sizes of nylon monofilament line: 20#, 40#, 80#, and 100#, at least 200 yards each. If you have room for only one spool, take the 40#.

Sinkers: Get a few torpedo sinkers with a brass eye at each end to get the bait down to the fish.

Wire: This is for tying on trolling lures. Get stranded wire, small enough to tie knots in. If you have enough room, get some for each size of line you have. Otherwise get 40#.

Handy-dandies: These are for catching bait and small scavengers. They consist of a few feet of line with four or five small hooks and some yarn or plastic. They are also known as Lucky Joes® or Lucky Luras®. Get several.

Scampis®: These are little rubber lures with floppy tails. You thread the tail onto a hook with a lead head. They can be trolled at raft-speed or thrown and retrieved. As far as I know, any fish with a big enough mouth will bite them.

Spinners, Spoons, and Such: There are many small lures that will catch fish. Pick up a few. Give preference to those with large, single hooks. Tiny hooks do not hold strong fish very well and you stand a good chance of ripping the raft or your hands on a treble hook. Give preference to those designed to work at slow speed.

Feather Lures, also known as barracuda feathers: These have a weighted head, a single hook, and a few feathers. Get a few.

Swivels: Get several of each of the sizes appropriate for 40# and 80# line. These are useful for tying ahead of a spinning lure and for securing heavy line to lighter line. If you are really pressed for space, so that half a cubic inch matters, you can leave these out.

Spear Gun: This saved Steve Callahan's life. Of course, he didn't have any other fishing gear. It must be considered a luxury, both in terms of money and space, but it sure would be nice to have. If I were the owner of a yacht crossing the ocean, I would spend the extra hundred dollars to save my own skin.

Get the kind that operates by rubber band rather than CO_2 cartridges, because rubber bands are reusable. Carry spare rubber bands. The smallest one is plenty big for your purposes.

Spear/Gaff: Dougal Robertson recommends a handle which will take either a spear head or gaff interchangeably. I have never seen one, but it sounds like a good idea. Maybe you can make one.

Spear Point and Doweling: This is not as good as the real thing, but it's cheaper and takes up less room. The doweling should be of a diameter that it will fit the spear shank after sharpening. It should be at least a foot long. Longer is better up to about 3½ or 4 feet. After that it will become hard to handle in a raft with an angry dorado attached to one end. Robertson recommends a six-foot spear, but he did all his successful fishing from an open dinghy rather than from a raft with a canopy.

The spear head should be two- or three-pointed, with barbs as large as possible. Dorado get violent when you stick them in the side with a spear, and small barbs can rip out of their skin. Sheathe the points, or wrap them in cloth, or stick pieces of styrofoam on them.

If you can, attach the head to the handle before packing it. Drill through the doweling for a secure hold. Fix a lanyard to the blunt end and loop it around your wrist or tie it to the raft. You cannot afford to lose your spear.

It wouldn't hurt to have spare parts.

FIRST AID

The Ship's Medicine Chest and Medical Aid at Sea recommends the following first aid kit for merchant vessels operating in cold water areas and unfrequented waterways. It is intended to be enough for 20-30 survivors for one week. This amounts to 10-15 survivors for two weeks, or 5-7 survivors for a month.

40 packages	Sunscreen to prevent sunburn
100 tablets	100 mg Acetaminophen, for minor aches or pain, antipyretic (fever reduction)
500 tablets	50 mg Cyclizine Hydrochloride for seasickness; mild antihistamine
100 tablets	1 g Sodium Chloride, for heat cramps
200 capsules	250 mg Tetracycline Hydrochloride broad spectrum antibiotic
100 capsules	100 mg Diphenylhydantoin Sodium anticonvulsant, antiepileptic
300 tablets	5 mg Diazepam, tranquilizer (Controlled Substance, Schedule III)
100 tablets	2.5 mg Diphenoxylate Hydrochloride and 0.025 mg Atropine Sulfate, antidiarrheal (Controlled Substance, Schedule V)

1 disposable cartridge 1 ml Epinephrine Hydrochloride 1:1000 injection asthmatic attack or difficulty in breathing after marine animal trauma

1 disposable cartridge 10 mg/ml, 1 ml Morphine Sulphate analgesic, sedative, (Controlled Substance, Schedule II)

(NOTE: Morphine must be locked up aboard ship. Only the captain and a delegated officer may be allowed access.)

12 rolls	4" elastic bandage
12 rolls	4" x 10 yards sterile gauze bandage
6 rolls	2" x 5 yards surgical adhesive tape
100 each	¾" x 3" adhesive bandages

200 each	4″ x 4″ sterile pads
2 bottles	insect repellent
1 pair	Lister bandage scissors
20 cakes	surgical soap

2 clinical fever thermometers

2 hypodermic syringe cartridge holders
(Get the syringe holder from the same supplier as the cartridges, to make sure they will fit.)

1 pair of sunglasses for each person

Substitutes for Controlled Substances:

If you do not have access to prescription drugs, you can substitute the following over-the-counter products for them.

Kaopectate® for diarrhea

Tylenol® with Codeine for morphine sulphate. Although this is a prescription drug, it is not nearly as tightly controlled a substance as morphine. Obey all control laws.

Here are a few more items it would be a good idea to have on hand:
Spare eye-glasses
2 bottles of an oil-based skin lotion, for salt-water boils
1 tube sulfadiazine silver cream, 1 per cent, for burns
1 tube ophthalmic ointment
1 package ammonia inhalants
1 bottle hydrogen peroxide, for cleaning wounds
1 bottle isopropyl alcohol, for cooling and for rashes

If you will be traveling in areas where sea snakes or the deadlier sorts of jellyfish live, you might want to add some antivenin. If you do take sea-snake antivenin, you must include some 1:1000 adrenalin, too, for allergic reactions.

TOOLS AND EQUIPMENT

Knife: A big, sturdy, folding knife with a locking blade or a sheath knife is a must. The one that comes with the raft is round-pointed and suitable only for cutting the painter. You will use the larger knife mostly for cleaning fish and for cutting it into strips for drying, but it has to be heavy enough to cut out the bottom shell of a turtle or the head off a small shark, if necessary. Get a good one.

Knife Sharpener: Any kind is all right. I like the ones which are a cylinder of diamond-impregnated steel. The metal scabbard screws onto the cylinder to become a handle. Dougal Robertson prefers the kind that has two sets of wheels. Be sure to make it small.

Extra Bailers: You may well need one at each end of the raft and an extra to use as a urinal so people will not have to climb over each other.

Extra Sponges: The raft probably already has one or two, but fish-gut acid can eat them up.

Cyalume® Light Sticks: These are plastic tubes about six inches long divided internally into two compartments full of different chemicals. When you bend the tube, a partition breaks, the chemicals mix, and they give off a bright green light that lasts several hours and makes no heat at all. You can use them for emergency light inside the raft or as a signal to rescuers. The only problem is that you cannot turn them off. They shine until the chemical reaction stops. Get half a dozen or more.

Spool of Nylon String: This has many uses, including fixing broken equipment, making gaffs and spears, and stringing fish out to dry. If you have room, get a couple of sizes.

Plywood: Two pieces of ⅛″ plywood, at least a foot square. Eighteen inches square would be better. You will need them for fish-cleaning boards because your raft is made of rubber, but they will have other uses as well, such as making an astrolabe to take star sights or to tie to a paddle to use as a rudder.

Heaving Line: Although your raft should already have one, get two 100′ coils of ¼″ polypropylene. You will use 50′ to troll with, 100′ as a trip line for your sea anchor, and 50′ as stays if you rig a sail.

<u>Hard Rubber Plugs</u>: Assorted sizes from one-inch diameter at the fat end to four-inch diameter. You will use these to plug holes in the raft. If you cannot find them, get wooden plugs.

<u>Hose Clamps</u>: Assorted sizes, one each per wooden plug. The most important use for these is to secure the edges of the hole in your raft around a wooden plug, but they can also be used to attach gaff hooks or spear points to doweling.

<u>Screwdriver</u> for the hose-clamps.

<u>Nippers and long-nosed Pliers</u>: These can be combined into one tool. They are for working with wire and taking hooks out of fish.

<u>Flashlight</u>: Equipped with long-shelf-life batteries, spare batteries and bulbs.

<u>Sewing Kit</u>, including needles for twine.

<u>Duct Tape</u>: If you are captain of a boat or ship, you already know that duct tape fixes anything.

<u>Silicon Sealant</u>: Get one small tube to repair the solar still.

<u>Stainless-steel Wire</u>: One coil for fixing broken equipment, such as spears.

<u>Aluminum Foil</u>: Take about ten feet off a roll and fold it as small as you can. This has several uses. You can make a light-weight radar reflector or a fishing lure, after sharks have taken all your store-bought ones.

NAVIGATION GEAR

How much navigation gear to include will depend on how much you know how to do and how much control you expect to have over your direction of travel. Keeping track of where you are drifting requires less accuracy than steering for a point of land.

Rather than pack a sextant, calculator, and such in the survival kit, you may want to try to grab your daily-use navigation gear on the way out the door. If so, you should make a habit of storing it in an easily accessible place near the hand-held VHF.

Magnetic Compass: Small plastic-bodied compasses are light and are good enough; you won't need accuracy to a tenth of a degree.

Watch: This should be digital and waterproof. Modern ones have lithium batteries good for seven years. Divers' watches are ideal. From time to time reset it according to a time tick from WWV or WWVH at 5000, 10,000, or 15,000 khz or from the BBC.

Charts of the area you will be cruising. These can be small scale. You will not have to know where you are within a mile. This book includes some pilot charts, but the page size limits their usefulness for plotting positions.

Writing Materials: Get enough paper, pencils and pens to keep a log as well as for navigation calculations.

Protractor: essential for calculating angles.

Dividers: These are nice but not essential. You can use them as spear points later.

Calculator: A very valuable modern convenience. It should have trig functions (tangent, cosine, sin, $\tan^{-1}$, $\cos^{-1}$, and $\sin^{-1}$). Most do nowadays. With a calculator, you can do any kind of navigation calculations with the formulas in the navigation chapter.

Two calculators are made for navigation. The one I like best is the Hewlett-Packard HP-41CX. This is a full-fledged hand-held computer with a navigation module that plugs in. It includes built-in tables, a perpetual Nautical Almanac, and a clock. The Tamaya NC-77 is good, but it requires that you have a watch, that you write down intermediate figures, and that you know the SHA and declinations of stars.

If you really have a lot of money, hand-held GPS (Global Positioning Systems) receivers exist. These give a continuous latitude and longitude readout from geosynchronous (stationary) satellites. They cost a couple of thousand dollars.

Sextant: This is useful only if you know how to use it. The cheapest plastic ones are good enough. The errors caused by being in a bouncing rubber raft at sea level are much greater than the sextant error.

This Book: It includes enough tables and explanation to get by.

READING MATERIAL

If you have prepared well and are lucky, you won't be cold, wet, thirsty, hungry, or in pain. You might well be scared, and you might well be bored. The following items will take care of both. You might want to read some of them beforehand.

Survive The Savage Sea, by Dougal Robertson. This is his narrative of his 38 days in a raft. He also wrote *Sea Survival—A Manual*, which is out of print. I have incorporated some of his ideas in this book.

Adrift, by Stephen Callahan. This one will let you know what you might still be in for and how to make the best of things. You will see what it is possible for a castaway to overcome. Reading of his matter-of-fact courage and tenacity will stiffen your spine.

Sole Survivor, by Ruthanne Lum McCunn. This is Poon Lim's story of 133 days alone on a wood-and-barrel raft in the Atlantic during World War II. He pulled a nail out of the planking with his teeth to make a fish hook and used a ration-can lid for a knife.

117 Days Adrift, by Maurice and Maralyn Bailey. This is another story of what you can do if you have wits and keep them about you. The Baileys kept alive (actually for 118 days) by catching fish with a safety pin and catching turtles with their hands.

The Captain's Guide To Liferaft Survival. You will have forgotten much of this by the time you end up in the water.

Be sure to include your own favorite book of religion, philosophy, puzzles, or watermaker repair.

THINGS TO HAVE IN CASE YOU WASH UP ON SHORE

Finger Saw: This is a foot-long piece of small–diameter, rough–textured cable with a finger-ring on each end. Use it to cut firewood and shelter–building materials. It takes up very little room.

Waterproof Matches and Candle: Use the matches to light the candle and the candle to light the fire. This saves matches for tomorrow. The candle can also be used to warm up a small shelter.

After you have put everything else in the bag, stuff in as much extra food and water as you can.

APPENDICES

FORMULAS, ALMANAC, TABLES

It is not posssible to be very accurate in a liferaft. It bounces too much to get a good reading from a sextant or a compass. For this reason, the tables that follow are simplified. For most purposes you can round numbers even more than they have been here, especially if you don't have a calculator.

Tables for the moon and planets are not included because they vary too rapidly and are too erratic for a long-term almanac to keep up with.

SOLAR ALMANAC

This is adapted from the long-term almanac in Volume 2 of Bowditch. It is based on the fact that any year's Nautical Almanac is more or less accurate if it is four years old, or eight years old, and so on. There are four columns in the table, for different years.

All figures are rounded to the nearest minute.

Figures are given for every third day, except at the end of 31-day months, when they are four days apart, and at the end of February, when they are 1 or 2 days apart.

The entries in the table are for Greenwich Hour Angle (GHA) for 0000 hours Greenwich. To interpolate for GHA at other times of day, add or subtract:

15 degrees for each hour,
15 minutes for each minute,
and 15 seconds for each second.

Interpolation for declination is linear in a particular week. Declination varies fastest at the equinoxes and slowest at the solstices.

Bowditch includes another correction, which has been eliminated here. It amounts to a maximum of a minute and a quarter every eight years, which is much too precise for lifeboats.

year 1989 1993 1997		year 1990 1994 1998		date	year 1991 1995 1999		year 1992 1996 2000 etc	
GHA	Dec	GHA	Dec		GHA	Dec	GHA	Dec
° ′	° ′	° ′	° ′	January	° ′	° ′	° ′	° ′
179 09	23 02S	179 11	23 03S	1	179 13	23 04S	179 14	23 06S
178 48	22 46S	178 50	22 47S	4	178 52	22 48S	178 53	22 50S
178 28	22 25S	178 30	22 27S	7	178 32	22 29S	178 33	22 31S
178 09	22 01S	178 11	22 03S	10	178 13	22 05S	178 13	22 07S
177 51	21 32S	177 53	21 35S	13	177 55	21 37S	177 58	21 40S
177 34	21 00S	177 37	21 03S	16	177 38	21 06S	177 39	21 09S
177 20	20 26S	177 22	20 28S	19	177 23	20 31S	177 24	20 34S
177 07	19 45S	177 09	19 49S	22	199 01	19 52S	177 10	19 57S
176 56	19 03S	176 57	19 06S	25	176 58	19 10S	176 58	19 14S
176 46	18 17S	176 47	18 21S	28	176 48	18 25S	176 48	18 29S
				February				
176 37	17 12S	176 37	17 16S	1	176 38	17 20S	176 38	17 25S
176 31	16 20S	176 31	16 24S	4	176 32	16 28S	176 32	16 33S
176 27	15 25S	176 28	15 29S	7	176 28	15 34S	176 28	15 39S
176 25	14 28S	176 26	14 33S	10	176 26	14 37S	176 26	14 43S
176 25	13 28S	176 26	13 34S	13	176 26	13 38S	176 25	13 44S
176 27	12 27S	176 28	12 32S	16	176 27	12 37S	176 27	12 43S
176 31	11 24S	176 31	11 29S	19	176 30	11 34S	176 30	11 40S
176 36	10 19S	176 35	10 25S	22	176 35	10 30S	176 34	10 36S
176 42	9 13S	176 42	9 19S	25	176 41	9 24S	176 40	9 30S
176 50	8 06S	176 49	8 11S	28	176 49	8 17S	176 47	8 23S
				March				
176 52	7 43S	176 52	7 49S	1	176 51	7 54S	176 53	7 38S
177 01	6 34S	177 01	6 40S	4	177 00	6 46S	177 02	6 29S
177 12	5 25S	177 11	5 31S	7	177 11	5 36S	177 13	5 19S
177 23	4 15S	177 20	4 20S	10	177 21	4 26S	177 24	4 09S
177 35	3 04S	177 34	3 10S	13	177 33	3 16S	177 36	2 58S
177 47	1 53S	177 46	1 59S	16	177 45	2 05S	177 48	1 47S
178 00	0 42S	177 59	0 48S	19	177 58	0 53S	178 01	0 36S
178 14	0 29N	178 13	0 24N	22	178 12	0 17N	178 15	0 35N
178 27	1 40N	178 26	1 35N	25	178 25	1 29N	178 28	1 46N
178 41	2 51N	178 40	2 45N	28	178 39	2 39N	178 42	2 57N

year 1989 1993 1997		1990 1994 1998		date	1991 1995 1999		1992 1996 2000 etc	
GHA	Dec	GHA	Dec		GHA	Dec	GHA	Dec
° ′	° ′	° ′	° ′	April	° ′	° ′	° ′	° ′
178 59	4 24N	178 58	4 19N	1	178 58	4 13N	179 00	4 30N
179 12	5 33N	179 11	5 28N	4	179 11	5 22N	179 13	5 39N
179 25	6 42N	179 24	6 36N	7	179 24	6 31N	179 26	6 47N
179 38	7 49N	179 37	7 44N	10	179 36	7 38N	179 39	7 54N
179 50	8 55N	179 49	8 50N	13	179 48	8 44N	179 51	9 00N
180 01	10 00N	180 00	9 55N	16	179 59	9 49N	180 02	10 05N
180 11	11 03N	180 11	10 58N	19	180 10	10 53N	180 12	11 08N
180 21	12 05N	180 20	12 00N	22	180 19	11 55N	180 21	12 10N
180 29	13 04N	180 29	13 00N	25	180 28	12 55N	180 30	13 09N
180 37	14 02N	180 36	13 58N	28	180 36	13 53N	180 37	14 07N
° ′	° ′	° ′	° ′	May	° ′	° ′	° ′	° ′
180 43	14 58N	180 42	14 54N	1	180 42	14 49N	180 43	15 03N
180 48	15 52N	180 48	15 48N	4	180 47	15 43N	180 48	15 56N
180 52	16 43N	180 51	16 39N	7	180 51	16 35N	180 52	16 47N
180 54	17 32N	180 54	17 28N	10	180 54	17 24N	180 55	17 36N
180 56	18 17N	180 56	18 14N	13	180 55	18 10N	180 56	18 21N
180 56	19 01N	180 56	18 58N	16	180 55	18 54N	180 55	19 05N
180 54	19 41N	180 54	19 38N	19	180 54	19 35N	180 54	19 45N
180 52	20 19N	180 52	20 16N	22	180 52	20 13N	180 51	20 22N
180 48	20 53N	180 48	20 51N	25	180 48	20 48N	180 48	20 56N
180 43	21 42N	180 43	21 22N	28	180 44	21 19N	180 43	21 27N
° ′	° ′	° ′	° ′	June	° ′	° ′	° ′	° ′
180 35	22 00N	180 35	21 58N	1	180 36	21 56N	180 35	22 02N
180 28	22 24N	180 28	21 22N	4	180 29	22 20N	180 27	22 25N
180 20	22 43N	180 20	22 42N	7	180 21	22 40N	180 19	22 45N
180 11	22 59N	180 12	22 58N	10	180 13	22 57N	180 11	23 00N
180 02	23 12N	180 03	23 11N	13	180 03	23 10N	180 02	23 12N
179 53	23 20N	179 53	23 20N	16	179 54	23 19N	179 52	23 21N
179 43	23 25N	179 44	23 25N	19	179 44	23 25N	179 42	23 26N
179 33	23 27N	179 34	23 27N	22	179 35	23 27N	179 32	23 27N
179 24	23 24N	179 24	23 24N	25	179 25	23 25N	179 23	23 24N
179 14	23 18N	179 15	23 19N	28	179 15	23 19N	179 13	23 17N

year	1989 1993 1997		1990 1994 1998			1991 1995 1999		1992 1996 2000 etc	
	GHA	Dec	GHA	Dec	date	GHA	Dec	GHA	Dec
					July				
	° ′	° ′	° ′	° ′		° ′	° ′	° ′	° ′
	179 05	23 08N	179 05	23 09N	1	179 06	23 10N	179 05	23 07N
	178 57	22 55N	178 57	22 59N	4	178 58	22 57N	178 56	22 54N
	178 49	22 38N	178 49	22 39N	7	178 50	22 41N	178 48	22 36N
	178 42	22 17N	178 42	22 19N	10	178 43	22 21N	178 42	22 15N
	178 36	21 53N	178 36	21 55N	13	178 36	21 57N	178 36	21 51N
	178 31	21 26N	178 31	21 28N	16	178 31	21 30N	178 31	21 23N
	178 27	20 55N	178 27	20 58N	19	178 27	21 00N	178 27	20 52N
	178 25	20 21N	178 25	20 39N	22	178 25	20 27N	178 25	20 18N
	178 24	19 44N	178 23	19 47N	25	178 23	19 50N	178 23	19 41N
	178 24	19 04N	178 23	19 08N	28	178 23	19 11N	178 24	19 01N
					August				
	178 26	19 07N	178 25	18 10N	1	178 25	18 14N	178 26	18 03N
	178 29	17 21N	178 28	17 24N	4	178 28	17 28N	178 29	17 17N
	178 33	16 32N	178 31	16 36N	7	178 32	16 40N	178 34	16 28N
	178 39	15 40N	178 39	15 45N	10	178 38	15 49N	178 40	15 36N
	178 47	14 47N	178 46	14 51N	13	178 45	14 57N	178 47	14 43N
	178 55	13 51N	178 54	13 56N	16	178 53	14 00N	178 56	13 46N
	179 05	12 54N	179 03	12 58N	19	179 03	13 03N	179 05	12 49N
	179 15	11 55N	179 14	11 59N	22	179 13	12 04N	179 16	11 50N
	179 27	10 53N	179 26	10 58N	25	179 25	11 03N	179 28	10 48N
	179 40	9 51N	179 38	9 56N	28	179 38	10 01N	179 41	9 46N
					September				
	179 58	8 25N	179 57	8 30N	1	179 56	8 35N	179 59	8 20N
	180 12	7 19N	180 11	7 24N	4	180 10	7 30N	180 14	7 14N
	180 27	6 12N	180 26	6 18N	7	180 25	6 23N	180 29	6 07N
	180 43	5 05N	180 41	5 10N	10	180 40	5 16N	180 44	4 59N
	180 59	3 56N	180 57	4 02N	13	180 56	4 07N	181 00	3 51N
	181 15	2 47N	182 13	2 53N	16	181 12	2 58N	182 16	2 42N
	181 31	1 38N	182 29	1 43N	19	181 27	1 49N	181 32	1 32N
	181 47	0 28N	182 45	0 33N	22	181 44	0 39N	181 48	0 22N
	182 02	0 43S	182 01	0 37S	25	182 00	0 31S	182 04	0 48S
	182 18	1 53S	182 16	1 57S	28	182 15	1 41S	182 19	1 58S

year	1989 1993 1997		1990 1994 1998			1991 1995 1999		1992 1996 2000 etc	
	GHA	Dec	GHA	Dec	date	GHA	Dec	GHA	Dec
	° ′	° ′	° ′	° ′	October	° ′	° ′	° ′	° ′
	182 32	3 03S	182 31	2 57S	1	182 30	2 51S	182 34	3 08S
	182 47	4 12S	182 45	4 07S	4	182 44	4 01S	182 48	4 18S
	183 00	5 22S	182 59	5 16S	7	182 58	5 11S	183 01	5 27S
	183 13	6.30S	183 12	6 25S	10	183 11	6 19S	183 14	6 36S
	183 24	7 38S	183 23	7 33S	13	183 22	7 27S	183 25	7 44S
	183 35	8 45S	183 34	8 40S	16	183 33	8 34S	183 35	8 51S
	183 44	9 51S	183 43	9 46S	19	183 42	9 40S	183 44	9 56S
	183 52	10 55S	183 51	10 50S	22	183 50	10 45S	183 52	11 01S
	183 58	11 59S	183 57	11 54S	25	183 57	11 48S	183 58	12 04S
	184 02	13 00S	184 02	12 55S	28	184 02	12 50S	184 03	13 05S
					November				
	184 06	14 19S	184 05	14 14S	1	184 05	14 09S	184 06	14 24S
	184 06	15 16S	184 06	15 11S	4	184 06	15 07S	184 06	15 20S
	184 05	16 10S	184 05	16 06S	7	184 05	16 03S	184 05	16 15S
	184 02	17 03S	184 03	16 59S	10	184 02	16 54S	184 01	17 07S
	183 57	17 52S	183 57	17 48S	13	183 57	17 44S	183 56	17 56S
	183 50	18 39S	183 50	18 35S	16	183 51	18 31S	183 49	18 43S
	183 41	19 23S	183 41	19 19S	19	183 42	19 16S	183 40	19 26S
	183 30	20 03S	183 31	20 00S	22	183 32	19 57S	183 29	20 07S
	183 17	20 41S	183 18	29 38S	25	183 19	20 35S	183 16	20 44S
	183 03	21 15S	183 04	21 12S	28	183 05	21 09S	183 02	21 17S
					December				
	182 47	21 45S	182 48	21 43S	1	182 50	21 40S	182 46	21 47S
	182 30	22 12S	182 31	22 09S	4	182 33	22 07S	182 28	22 14S
	182 11	22 34S	182 13	22 32S	7	183 14	22 31S	182 09	22 36S
	181 51	22 53S	181 53	22 51S	10	181 54	22 50S	181 49	22 54S
	181 31	23 07S	181 32	23 06S	13	181 34	23 05S	181 29	23 08S
	181 09	23 18S	181 11	23 17S	16	181 12	23 17S	181 07	23 19S
	180 47	23 24S	180 49	23 24S	19	180 51	23 24S	180 45	23 25S
	180 25	23 27S	180 27	23 27S	22	180 28	23 26S	180 23	23 27S
	180 02	23 24S	180 04	23 25S	25	180 06	23 25S	180 00	23 24S
	179 40	23 18S	179 42	23 19S	28	179 44	23 19S	179 38	23 18S

STAR ALMANAC

GHA of Aries

Numbers given are the GHA of the first point of Aries for 0 hours on the first day of each month.

For other days and other times, add:

> 0 degrees 59.14 minutes per day
> 15 degrees 02.5 minutes per hour
> 15 minutes per minute
> 15 seconds per second.

To make these interpolations easier, use the multiplication table on page 159.

1989 1993 1997	1990 1994 1998		1991 1995 1999	1992 1996 2000 etc
° ′	° ′		° ′	° ′
100 38	100 24	Jan	100 09	99 53
131 11	130 57	Feb	130 43	130 26
158 47	158 33	Mar	158 18	159 01
189 20	189 05	Apr	188 51	189 34
218 54	218 39	May	218 25	219 08
249 27	249 14	Jun	248 59	249 42
279 02	278 48	Jul	278 33	279 16
309 35	309 21	Aug	309 07	309 50
340 08	339 54	Sep	339 39	340 22
9 42	9 28	Oct	9 14	9 57
40 16	40 02	Nov	39 48	40 31
69 50	69 36	Dec	69 22	70 05

GHA star = GHA Aries + SHA star

SHA AND DECLINATION OF SELECTED STARS

This table is correct for 1989. For later years multiply the annual corrections by the number of years after 1989, and add the answers to the SHA and the declination.

Figures are given to the nearest tenth of a minute. This is more accuracy than you will need in a liferaft, but this way the number will round correctly to the nearest minute when a correction is added.

SHA	SHA Corr	Star	Declination	Dec Corr
° ′	° ′		° ′	° ′
315 31.9	− 0.57	Acamar	S40 21.0	− 0.24
335 40.0	− 0.56	Achernar	S57 17.7	− 0.30
173 30.3	− 0.84	Acrux	S63 02.1	+ 0.33
291 10.3	− 0.86	Aldebaran	N16 29.4	+ 0.12
153 13.3	− 0.59	Alkaid	N49 21.7	− 0.30
218 13.9	− 0.74	Alphard	S 8 36.6	+ 0.26
126 26.8	− 0.64	Alphecca	N26 44.8	− 0.20
358 02.8	− 0.78	Alpheratz	N29 02.0	+ 0.33
62 26.5	− 0.73	Altair	N 8 50.2	+ 0.16
112 49.2	− 0.92	Antares	S26 24.6	+ 0.13
146 12.6	− 0.68	Arcturus	N19 14.1	− 0.31
108 08.3	− 1.59	Atria	S69 00.5	+ 0.11
271 20.9	− 0.81	Betelgeuse	N 7 24.5	+ 0.01
264 03.8	− 0.33	Canopus	S52 41.3	+ 0.03
281 01.3	− 1.11	Capella	N45 59.5	+ 0.06
49 44.6	− 0.51	Deneb	N45 14.5	+ 0.22
182 52.3	− 0.76	Denebola	N14 37.9	− 0.34
349 14.3	− 0.75	Diphda	S18 02.9	− 0.33
194 13.5	− 0.92	Dubhe	N61 48.3	− 0.32
34 05.5	− 0.74	Enif	N 9 49.4	+ 0.28

SHA	SHA Corr	Star	Declination	Dec Corr
° ′	° ′		° ′	° ′
15 44.3	−0.83	Fomalhaut	S29 41.0	−0.32
328 21.5	−0.85	Hamal	N23 24.9	+0.28
137 19.4	+0.04	Kochab	N74 11.6	−0.25
148 29.6	−0.88	Menkent	S36 18.9	+0.29
309 06.6	−1.07	Mirfak	N49 49.7	+0.21
76 21.5	−0.93	Nunki	S26 18.8	-0.08
53 48.5	−1.18	Peacock	S56 46.5	−0.19
243 49.8	−0.92	Pollux	N28 03.2	−0.15
245 18.6	−0.78	Procyon	N 5 15.3	−0.16
96 23.9	−0.70	Rasalhague	N12 33.9	−0.04
208 02.8	−0.80	Regulus	N12 01.2	−0.29
281 29.4	−0.72	Rigel	S 8 12.7	−0.07
140 17.5	−1.02	Rigel Kent.	S60 47.2	+0.25
350 01.9	−0.86	Schedar	N56 29.0	+0.33
258 49.6	−0.66	Sirius	S16 42.0	+0.08
158 50.8	−0.79	Spica	S11 06.3	+0.31
223 05.8	−0.55	Suhail	S43 23.1	+0.24
80 51.9	−0.51	Vega	N38 46.2	+0.06

MULTIPLICATION TABLE

No.	°	° ′	′	° ′	° ′	° ′	° ′
1	15	0 15	0.2	1.8	0 59.1	15 02.5	0 15.0
2	30	0 30	0.5	3.7	1 58.3	30 04.9	0 30.1
3	45	0 45	0.8	5.5	2 57.4	45 07.4	0 45.1
4	60	1 00	1.0	7.4	3 56.6	60 09.9	1 00.2
5	75	1 15	1.2	9.2	4 55.7	75 12.3	1 15.2
6	90	1 30	1.5	11.0	5 54.8	90 14.8	1 30.2
7	105	1 45	1.8	12.9	6 54.0	105 17.2	1 45.3
8	120	2 00	2.0	14.7	7 53.1	120 19.7	2 00.3
9	135	2 15	2.2	16.6	8 52.3	135 22.2	2 15.4
10	150	2 30	2.5	18.4	9 51.4	150 24.6	2 30.4
11	165	2 45	2.8	20.2	10 50.5	165 27.1	2 45.5
12	180	3 00	3.0	22.1	11 49.7	180 29.6	3 00.5
13	195	3 15	3.2	23.9	12 48.8	195 32.0	3 15.5
14	210	3 30	3.5	25.8	13 48.0	210 34.5	3 30.6
15	225	3 45	3.8	27.6	14 47.1	225 37.0	3 45.6
16	240	4 00	4.0	29.4	15 46.2	240 39.4	4 00.7
17	255	4 15	4.2	31.3	16 45.4	255 41.9	4 15.7
18	270	4 30	4.5	33.1	17 44.5	270 44.4	4 30.7
19	285	4 45	4.8	35.0	18 43.7	285 46.8	4 45.8
20	300	5 00	5.0	36.8	19 42.8	300 49.3	5 00.8
21	315	5 15	5.2	38.6	20 41.9	315 51.7	5 15.9
22	330	5 30	5.5	40.5	21 41.1	330 54.2	5 30.9
23	345	5 45	5.8	42.3	22 40.2	345 56.7	5 45.9
24	360	6 00	6.0	44.2	23 39.4	360 59.1	6 01.0
25	---	6 15	6.2	46.0	24 38.5	--------	6 16.0
26	---	6 30	6.5	47.8	25 37.6	--------	6 31.1
27	---	6 45	6.8	49.7	26 36.8	--------	6 46.1
28	---	7 00	7.0	51.5	27 35.9	--------	7 01.1
29	---	7 15	7.2	53.4	28 35.1	--------	7 16.2
30	---	7 30	7.5	55.2	29 34.2	--------	7 31.2

No.	°	° '	'	° '	° '	° '	° '
31	---	7 45	7.8	57.0	30 33.3	--------	7 46.3
32	---	8 00	8.0	58.9	-------	--------	8 01.3
33	---	8 15	8.2	60.7	-------	--------	8 16.4
34	---	8 30	8.5	62.6	-------	--------	8 31.4
35	---	8 45	8.8	64.4	-------	--------	8 46.4
36	---	9 00	9.0	66.2	-------	--------	9 01.5
37	---	9 15	9.2	68.1	-------	--------	9 16.5
38	---	9 30	9.5	69.9	-------	--------	9 31.6
39	---	9 45	9.8	71.8	-------	--------	9 46.6
40	---	10 00	10.0	73.6	-------	--------	10 01.6
41	---	10 15	10.2	75.4	-------	--------	10 16.7
42	---	10 30	10.5	77.3	-------	--------	10 31.7
43	---	10 45	10.8	79.1	-------	--------	10 46.8
44	---	11 00	11.0	81.0	-------	--------	11 01.8
45	---	11 15	11.2	82.8	-------	--------	11 16.8
46	---	11 30	11.5	84.8	-------	--------	11 31.9
47	---	11 45	11.8	86.5	-------	--------	11 46.9
48	---	12 00	12.0	88.3	-------	--------	12 02.0
49	---	12 15	12.2	90.2	-------	--------	12 17.0
50	---	12 30	12.5	92.0	-------	--------	12 32.1
51	---	12 45	12.8	93.8	-------	--------	12 47.1
52	---	13 00	13.0	95.7	-------	--------	13 02.1
53	---	13 15	13.2	97.5	-------	--------	13 17.2
54	---	13 30	13.5	99.4	-------	--------	13 32.2
55	---	13 45	13.8	----	-------	--------	13 47.3
56	---	14 00	14.0	----	-------	--------	14 02.3
57	---	14 15	14.2	----	-------	--------	14 17.3
58	---	14 30	14.5	----	-------	--------	14 32.4
59	---	14 45	14.8	----	-------	--------	14 47.4
60	---	15 00	15.0	----	-------	--------	15 02.5

DECIMAL PARTS OF DAY AND YEAR

0.0	0.1	0.2	0.3	0.4	0.5	0.6	0.7	0.8	0.9	1.0
0000 to 0112	0112 to 0336	0336 to 0600	0600 to 0824	0824 to 1048	1048 to 1312	1312 to 1536	1536 to 1800	1800 to 2024	2024 to 2248	2248 to 2400
Jan1 to Jan18	Jan19 to Feb23	Feb24 to Apr1	Apr2 to May7	May8 to Jun13	Jun14 to Jul19	Jul20 to Aug25	Aug26 to Sep30	Oct1 to Nov6	Nov7 to Dec12	Dec13 to Dec31

LOCAL STANDARD ZONE TIME
CONVERTED TO GREENWICH MEAN TIME

007.5W -007.5E	Local zone time	= GMT
007.5E - 022.5E	Local zone time − 1	= GMT
022.5E - 037.5E	Local zone time − 2	= GMT
037.5E - 052.5E	Local zone time − 3	= GMT
052.5E - 067.5E	Local zone time − 4	= GMT
067.5E - 082.5E	Local zone time − 5	= GMT
082.5E - 097.5E	Local zone time − 6	= GMT
097.5E - 112.5E	Local zone time − 7	= GMT
112.5E - 127.5E	Local zone time − 8	= GMT
127.5E - 142.5E	Local zone time − 9	= GMT
142.5E - 157.5E	Local zone time − 10	= GMT
157.5E - 172.5E	Local zone time − 11	= GMT
172.5E - 180	Local zone time − 12	= GMT
180 - 172.5W	Local zone time + 12	= GMT
172.5W - 157.5W	Local zone time + 11	= GMT
157.5W - 142.5W	Local zone time + 10	= GMT
142.5W - 127.5W	Local zone time + 9	= GMT
127.5W - 112.5W	Local zone time + 8	= GMT

112.5W - 097.5W	Local zone time + 7	= GMT
097.5W - 082.5W	Local zone time + 6	= GMT
082.5W - 067.5W	Local zone time + 5	= GMT
067.5W - 052.5W	Local zone time + 4	= GMT
052.5W - 037.5W	Local zone time + 3	= GMT
037.5W - 022.5W	Local zone time + 2	= GMT
022.5W - 007.5W	Local zone time + 1	= GMT
007.5W - 007.5E	Local zone time	= GMT

CELESTIAL FORMULAS

Explanations are found in Chapter 10.

Abbreviations:

A = amplitude
d = declination of the body
L = your DR latitude; your assumed latitude
Hc = computed altitude; the altitude the body would be in the sky if you
    were really at your assumed position.
Z = azimuth

GHA = Greenwich Hour Angle; angular distance west of Greenwich.
SHA = Sidereal Hour Angle; angular distance of the star west of the
    first point of Aries.
GHA star = GHA Aries + SHA star. This is always plus.
LHA = Local Hour Angle; angular distance west of your position.
LHA = GHA + east longitude.
    or GHA − west longitude.

If you are using a calculator, remember that everything must be entered as decimals. Degrees and minutes must be entered as decimal degrees. Minutes and seconds must be entered as decimal minutes.

Amplitudes

$$A = \sin^{-1} \left(\frac{\sin d}{\cos L} \right)$$

All terms are positive, even if latitude and declination are different names (one north and one south).

The answer this gives you is an amplitude, not yet a bearing. It is the angle of the body north or south from east or west of you.

The amplitude is east when the body is rising
west when the body is setting
north of E or W when the declination is north
south of E or W when the declination is south.

AMPLITUDES

Enter the table with your latitude north or south and the declination of the body north or south, and interpolate to find the amplitude of the body.

Declination N or S

		0	5	10	15	20	25	29
	0	0	5	10	15	20	25	29
	10	0	5.1	10.2	15.3	20.3	25.4	29.5
	20	0	5.3	10.7	15.9	21.4	26.7	31.1
Latitude	30	0	5.8	11.6	17.4	23.3	29.2	34.1
N or S	40	0	6.5	13.1	19.8	26.5	33.5	39.5
	45	0	8.5	14.2	21.5	28.9	36.7	43.3
	50	0	9.4	15.7	23.8	32.2	41.1	49.0
	55	0	10.5	17.6	26.8	36.6	47.5	57.7
	60	0	12.1	20.3	31.2	43.2	57.7	75.8
	62.5	0	13.1	22.1	34.1	47.8	66.2	----

SIGHT REDUCTION

For all three of the following formulas, if latitude and declination are contrary names (one north and one south), enter the declination as a negative number.

Computed Altitude Formula

$$Hc = \sin^{-1}[(\sin L \sin d) + (\cos L \cos d \cos LHA)]$$

Azimuths (bearings of celestial bodies)

In both formulas, if the latitude and declination are of contrary name (one north and one south), enter the declination as a negative number.

If the LHA is greater than 180, enter it as a negative number.

If the answer you get is negative, add 180 to it.

Your answer will be an azimuth angle, up to 180 east or west from north or south. The azimuth angle starts from the north when you are in northern latitudes and from the south when you are in southern latitudes. It goes east or west according to which side of your meridian the body is on.

Time Azimuth Formula

$$Z = \tan^{-1}\left(\frac{\sin LHA}{(\cos L \tan d) - (\sin L \cos LHA)}\right)$$

Altitude Azimuth Formula

To use this method, you must first find the computed altitude (Hc).

$$Z = \cos^{-1}\left(\frac{\sin d - (\sin L \sin Hc)}{(\cos L \cos Hc)}\right)$$

Cross-Staff Observation Formulas

Full cross-staff:

$$\text{Altitude} = 2\tan^{-1}\left(\frac{x}{y}\right)$$

Half cross staff:

$$\text{Altitude} = \tan^{-1}\left(\frac{x}{y}\right)$$

STAR REFRACTION TABLE

Alt	5	6	7	8	10	12	15	21	33	63	90
Refr	9′	8′	7′	6′	5′	4′	3′	2′	1′	0	

Dip in minutes = square root of the height of the eye in feet.

Semidiameter correction = 16′ plus for lower limb; minus for upper limb. Ignore this correction with an astrolabe.

MERCATOR SAILINGS

SIMPLIFIED TRAVERSE TABLE

Course Angle	0	18	31	41	49	56	63	75	81	87	90
Factor	1.0	0.9	0.8	0.7	0.6	0.5	0.4	0.3	0.2	0.0	

To find your change in latitude, enter the table with your course angle. Course angle is explained on page 101.

Multiply the course angle by the factor below it.

The answer is your change in latitude, in minutes.

To find your change in longitude, subtract your course angle from 90, and use that to enter the table. Multiply the factor by distance run. This gives you the departure.

Enter the table again with the midlatitude, that is, latitude between your start and finish. Divide your departure by the factor below your latitude. This gives you the change in longitude.

Change in Latitude by Formula

Change in latitude = Distance traveled times the cosine of the course angle.

Distance is entered in nautical miles.

Change in Longitude by Formula and Table

Change Long. = (tan Course Angle * Change Lat. * Factor in the following table)

Latitude	0	18	29	36	41	46	49	52	54	56	58	60
Factor	1.0	1.1	1.2	1.3	1.4	1.5	1.6	1.7	1.8	1.9	2.0	

MISCELLANEOUS FORMULAS

Distance to the real horizon in nautical miles = square root of the height of the eye in feet times 1.06.

Distance to the visible horizon = square root of the height of the eye in feet times 1.14.

Distance to the radar horizon = square root of the height of the radar times 1.22.

The difference is due to refraction of light and radio waves.

NATURAL TRIGONOMETRIC FUNCTIONS

This table is extremely condensed. Without interpolation, it will give accuracy within a degree for azimuths and bearings. Computed altitude will be accurate within about 18 minutes. Interpolate for better accuracy. For degrees higher than 180, sin, cos, and tan are negative.

Degrees	Degrees	Degrees	Degrees	Sin	Cos	Tan
0.0	180.0	180.0	270.0	0.0000	1.0000	0.0000
0.5	179.5	180.5	270.5	0.0087	1.0000	0.0087
1.0	179.0	181.0	271.0	0.0175	0.9998	0.0175
1.5	178.5	181.5	271.5	0.0262	0.9997	0.0262
2.0	178.0	182.0	272.0	0.0349	0.9994	0.0349
2.5	177.5	182.5	272.5	0.0436	0.9990	0.0437
3.0	177.0	183.0	273.0	0.0523	0.9986	0.0524
3.5	176.5	183.5	273.5	0.0610	0.9981	0.0612
4.0	176.0	184.0	274.0	0.0698	0.9976	0.0699
4.5	175.5	184.5	274.5	0.0785	0.9969	0.0787
5.0	175.0	185.0	275.0	0.0872	0.9962	0.0875
5.5	174.5	185.5	275.5	0.0958	0.9954	0.0963
6.0	174.0	186.0	276.0	0.1045	0.9945	0.1051
6.5	173.5	186.5	276.5	0.1132	0.9936	0.1139
7.0	173.0	187.0	277.0	0.1219	0.9925	0.1228
7.5	172.5	187.5	277.5	0.1305	0.9914	0.1317
8.0	172.0	188.0	278.0	0.1392	0.9903	0.1405
8.5	171.5	188.5	278.5	0.1478	0.9890	0.1495
9.0	171.0	189.0	279.0	0.1564	0.9877	0.1584

Degrees	Degrees	Degrees	Degrees	Sin	Cos	Tan
9.5	170.5	189.5	279.5	0.1650	0.9863	0.1673
10.0	170.0	190.0	280.0	0.1736	0.9848	0.1763
10.5	169.5	190.5	280.5	0.1822	0.9833	0.1853
11.0	169.0	191.0	281.0	0.1908	0.9816	0.1944
11.5	168.5	191.5	281.5	0.1994	0.9799	0.2035
12.0	168.0	192.0	282.0	0.2079	0.9781	0.2126
12.5	167.5	192.5	282.5	0.2164	0.9763	0.2217
13.0	167.0	193.0	283.0	0.2250	0.9744	0.2300
13.5	166.5	193.5	283.5	0.2334	0.9724	0.2401
14.0	166.0	194.0	284.0	0.2419	0.9703	0.2493
14.5	165.5	194.5	284.5	0.2504	0.9681	0.2586
15.0	165.0	195.0	285.0	0.2588	0.9659	0.2679
15.5	164.5	195.5	285.5	0.2672	0.9636	0.2773
16.0	164.0	196.0	286.0	0.2756	0.9613	0.2867
16.5	163.5	196.5	286.5	0.2840	0.9588	0.2962
17.0	163.0	197.0	287.0	0.2924	0.9563	0.3057
17.5	162.5	197.5	287.5	0.3007	0.9537	0.3153
18.0	162.0	198.0	288.0	0.3090	0.9511	0.3249
18.5	161.5	198.5	288.5	0.3173	0.9483	0.3346
19.0	161.0	199.0	289.0	0.3256	0.9455	0.3443
19.5	160.5	199.5	289.5	0.3338	0.9426	0.3541
20.0	160.0	200.0	290.0	0.3420	0.9397	0.3640
20.5	159.5	200.5	290.5	0.3502	0.9367	0.3739
21.0	159.0	201.0	291.0	0.3584	0.9336	0.3839
21.5	158.5	201.5	291.5	0.3665	0.9304	0.3939
22.0	158.0	202.0	292.0	0.3746	0.9272	0.4040
22.5	157.5	202.5	292.5	0.3827	0.9239	0.4142
23.0	157.0	203.0	293.0	0.3907	0.9205	0.4245
23.5	156.5	203.5	293.5	0.3987	0.9171	0.4348
24.0	156.0	204.0	294.0	0.4067	0.9135	0.4452
24.5	155.5	204.5	294.5	0.4147	0.9100	0.4557
25.0	155.0	205.0	295.0	0.4226	0.9063	0.4663
25.5	154.5	205.5	295.5	0.4305	0.9026	0.4770
26.0	154.0	206.0	296.0	0.4384	0.8988	0.4877
26.5	153.5	206.5	296.5	0.4462	0.8949	0.4986
27.0	153.0	207.0	297.0	0.4540	0.8910	0.5095
27.5	152.5	207.5	297.5	0.4617	0.8870	0.5206
28.0	152.0	208.0	298.0	0.4695	0.8829	0.5317
28.5	151.5	208.5	298.5	0.4772	0.8788	0.5430
29.0	151.0	209.0	299.0	0.4848	0.8746	0.5543
29.5	150.5	209.5	299.5	0.4924	0.8704	0.5658
30.0	150.0	210.0	300.0	0.5000	0.8660	0.5774

Degrees	Degrees	Degrees	Degrees	Sin	Cos	Tan
30.5	149.5	210.5	300.5	0.5075	0.8616	0.5890
31.0	149.0	211.0	301.0	0.5150	0.8572	0.6009
31.5	148.5	211.5	301.5	0.5225	0.8526	0.6128
32.0	148.0	212.0	302.0	0.5299	0.8480	0.6249
32.5	147.5	212.5	302.5	0.5373	0.8434	0.6371
33.0	147.0	213.0	303.0	0.5446	0.8387	0.6494
33.5	146.5	213.5	303.5	0.5519	0.8339	0.6619
34.0	146.0	214.0	304.0	0.5592	0.8290	0.6745
34.5	145.5	214.5	304.5	0.5664	0.8241	0.6873
35.0	145.0	215.0	305.0	0.5736	0.8192	0.7002
35.5	144.5	215.5	305.5	0.5807	0.8141	0.7133
36.0	144.0	216.0	306.0	0.5878	0.8090	0.7265
36.5	143.5	216.5	306.5	0.5948	0.8039	0.7400
37.0	143.0	217.0	307.0	0.6018	0.7986	0.7536
37.5	142.5	217.5	307.5	0.6088	0.7934	0.7673
38.0	142.0	218.0	308.0	0.6157	0.7880	0.7813
38.5	141.5	218.5	308.5	0.6225	0.7826	0.7954
39.0	141.0	219.0	309.0	0.6293	0.7771	0.8098
39.5	140.5	219.5	309.5	0.6361	0.7716	0.8243
40.0	140.0	220.0	310.0	0.6428	0.7660	0.8391
40.5	139.5	220.5	310.5	0.6494	0.7604	0.8541
41.0	139.0	221.0	311.0	0.6561	0.7547	0.8693
41.5	138.5	221.5	311.5	0.6626	0.7490	0.8847
42.0	138.0	222.0	312.0	0.6691	0.7431	0.9004
42.5	137.5	222.5	312.5	0.6756	0.7373	0.9163
43.0	137.0	223.0	313.0	0.6820	0.7314	0.9325
43.5	136.5	223.5	313.5	0.6884	0.7254	0.9490
44.0	136.0	224.0	314.0	0.6947	0.7193	0.9657
44.5	135.5	224.5	314.5	0.7009	0.7133	0.9827
45.0	135.0	225.0	315.0	0.7071	0.7071	1.0000
45.5	134.5	225.5	315.5	0.7133	0.7009	1.0176
46.0	134.0	226.0	316.0	0.7193	0.6947	1.0355
46.5	133.5	226.5	316.5	0.7254	0.6884	1.0538
47.0	133.0	227.0	317.0	0.7314	0.6820	1.0724
47.5	132.5	227.5	317.5	0.7373	0.6756	1.0913
48.0	132.0	228.0	318.0	0.7431	0.6691	1.1106
48.5	131.5	228.5	318.5	0.7490	0.6626	1.1303
49.0	131.0	229.0	319.0	0.7547	0.6561	1.1504
49.5	130.5	229.5	319.5	0.7604	0.6494	1.1708
50.0	130.0	230.0	320.0	0.7660	0.6428	1.1918
50.5	129.5	230.5	320.5	0.7716	0.6361	1.2131
51.0	129.0	231.0	321.0	0.7771	0.6293	1.2349

Degrees	Degrees	Degrees	Degrees	Sin	Cos	Tan
51.5	128.5	231.5	321.5	0.7826	0.6225	1.2572
52.0	128.0	232.0	322.0	0.7880	0.6157	1.2799
52.5	127.5	232.5	322.5	0.7934	0.6088	1.3032
53.0	127.0	233.0	323.0	0.7986	0.6018	1.3270
53.5	126.5	233.5	323.5	0.8039	0.5948	1.3514
54.0	126.0	234.0	324.0	0.8090	0.5878	1.3764
54.5	125.5	234.5	324.5	0.8141	0.5807	1.4019
55.0	125.0	235.0	325.0	0.8192	0.5736	1.4281
55.5	124.5	235.5	325.5	0.8241	0.5664	1.4550
56.0	124.0	236.0	326.0	0.8290	0.5592	1.4826
56.5	123.5	236.5	326.5	0.8339	0.5519	1.5108
57.0	123.0	237.0	327.0	0.8387	0.5446	1.5399
57.5	122.5	237.5	327.5	0.8434	0.5373	1.5697
58.0	122.0	238.0	328.0	0.8480	0.5299	1.6003
58.5	121.5	238.5	328.5	0.8526	0.5225	1.6319
59.0	121.0	239.0	329.0	0.8572	0.5150	1.6643
59.5	120.5	239.5	329.5	0.8616	0.5075	1.6977
60.0	120.0	240.0	330.0	0.8660	0.5000	1.7321
60.5	119.5	240.5	330.5	0.8704	0.4924	1.7675
61.0	119.0	241.0	331.0	0.8746	0.4848	1.8040
61.5	118.5	241.5	331.5	0.8788	0.4772	1.8418
62.0	118.0	242.0	332.0	0.8829	0.4695	1.8807
62.5	117.5	242.5	332.5	0.8870	0.4617	1.9210
63.0	117.0	243.0	333.0	0.8910	0.4540	1.9626
63.5	116.5	243.5	333.5	0.8949	0.4462	2.0057
64.0	116.0	244.0	334.0	0.8988	0.4384	2.0503
64.5	115.5	244.5	334.5	0.9026	0.4305	2.0965
65.0	115.0	245.0	335.0	0.9063	0.4226	2.1445
65.5	114.5	245.5	335.5	0.9100	0.4147	2.1943
66.0	114.0	246.0	336.0	0.9135	0.4067	2.2460
66.5	113.5	246.5	336.5	0.9171	0.3987	2.2998
67.0	113.0	247.0	337.0	0.9205	0.3907	2.3559
67.5	112.5	247.5	337.5	0.9239	0.3827	2.4142
68.0	112.0	248.0	338.0	0.9272	0.3746	2.4751
68.5	111.5	248.5	338.5	0.9304	0.3665	2.5386
69.0	111.0	249.0	339.0	0.9336	0.3584	2.6051
69.5	110.5	249.5	339.5	0.9367	0.3502	2.6746
70.0	110.0	250.0	340.0	0.9397	0.3420	2.7475
70.5	109.5	250.5	340.5	0.9426	0.3338	2.8239
71.0	109.0	251.0	341.0	0.9455	0.3256	2.9042
71.5	108.5	251.5	341.5	0.9483	0.3173	2.9887
72.0	108.0	252.0	342.0	0.9511	0.3090	3.0777

Degrees	Degrees	Degrees	Degrees	Sin	Cos	Tan
72.5	107.5	252.5	342.5	0.9537	0.3007	3.1716
73.0	107.0	253.0	343.0	0.9563	0.2924	3.2709
73.5	106.5	253.5	343.5	0.9588	0.2840	3.3759
74.0	106.0	254.0	344.0	0.9613	0.2756	3.4874
74.5	105.5	254.5	344.5	0.9636	0.2672	3.6059
75.0	105.0	255.0	345.0	0.9659	0.2588	3.7321
75.5	104.5	255.5	345.5	0.9681	0.2504	3.8667
76.0	104.0	256.0	346.0	0.9703	0.2419	4.0108
76.5	103.5	256.5	346.5	0.9724	0.2334	4.1653
77.0	103.0	257.0	347.0	0.9744	0.2250	4.3315
77.5	102.5	257.5	347.5	0.9763	0.2164	4.5107
78.0	102.0	258.0	348.0	0.9781	0.2079	4.7046
78.5	101.5	258.5	348.5	0.9799	0.1994	4.9152
79.0	101.0	259.0	349.0	0.9816	0.1908	5.1446
79.5	100.5	259.5	349.5	0.9833	0.1822	5.3955
80.0	100.0	260.0	350.0	0.9848	0.1736	5.6713
80.5	99.5	260.5	350.5	0.9863	0.1650	5.9758
81.0	99.0	261.0	351.0	0.9877	0.1564	6.3138
81.5	98.5	261.5	351.5	0.9890	0.1478	6.6912
82.0	98.0	262.0	352.0	0.9903	0.1392	7.1154
82.5	97.5	262.5	352.5	0.9914	0.1305	7.5958
83.0	97.0	263.0	353.0	0.9925	0.1219	8.1443
83.5	96.5	263.5	353.5	0.9936	0.1132	8.7769
84.0	96.0	264.0	354.0	0.9945	0.1045	9.514ᴧ
84.5	95.5	264.5	354.5	0.9954	0.0958	10.3854
85.0	95.0	265.0	355.0	0.9962	0.0872	11.4301
85.5	94.5	265.5	355.5	0.9969	0.0785	12.7062
86.0	94.0	266.0	356.0	0.9976	0.0698	14.3007
86.5	93.5	266.5	356.5	0.9981	0.0610	16.3499
87.0	93.0	267.0	357.0	0.9986	0.0523	19.0811
87.5	92.5	267.5	357.5	0.9990	0.0436	22.9038
88.0	92.0	268.0	358.0	0.9994	0.0349	28.6363
88.5	91.5	268.5	358.5	0.9997	0.0262	38.1885
89.0	91.0	269.0	359.0	0.0998	0.0175	57.2900
89.5	90.5	269.5	359.5	1.0000	0.0087	114.5887
90.0	90.0	270.0	360.0	1.0000	0.0000	infinity

STARS IN THE VICINITY OF CYGNUS

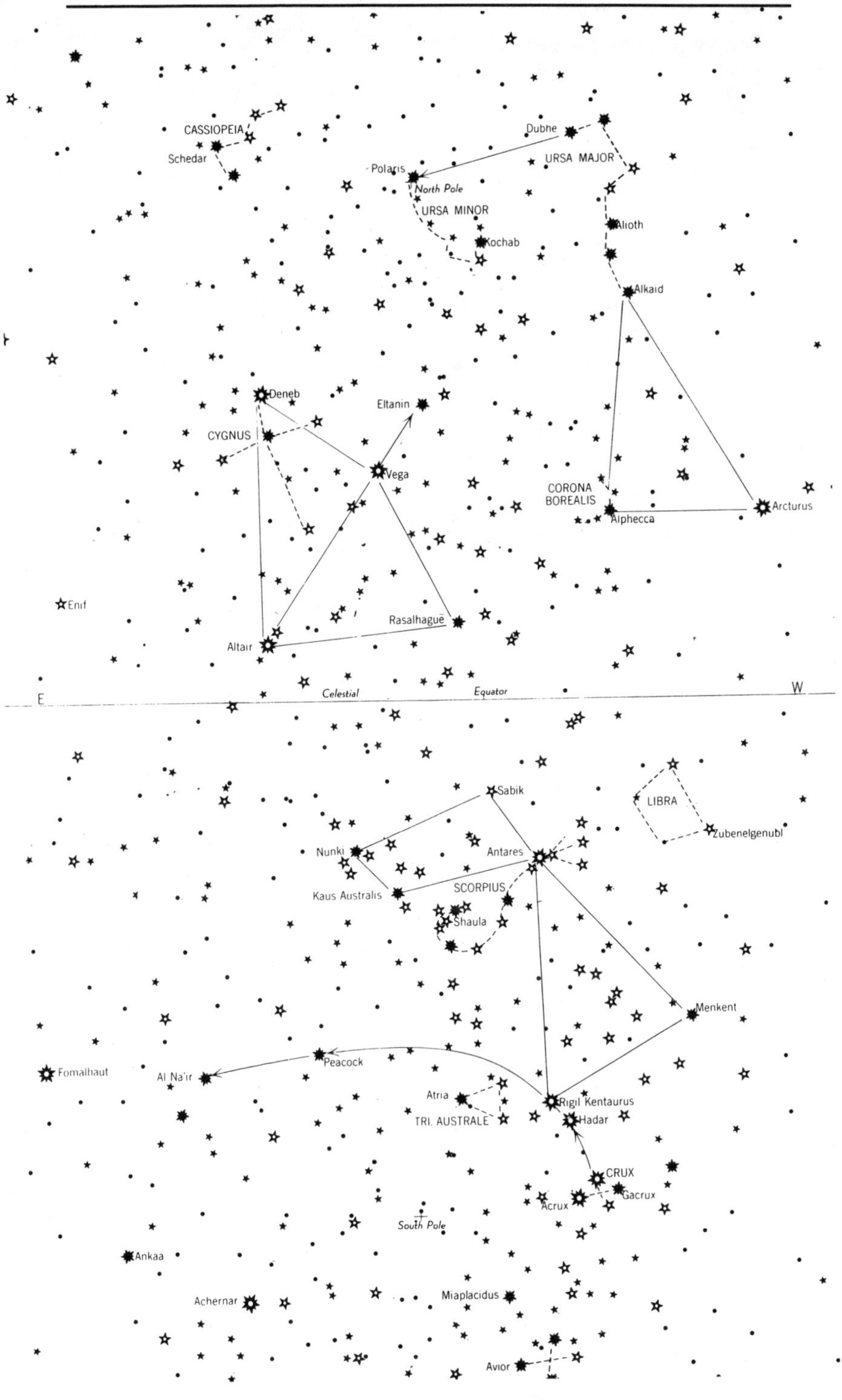

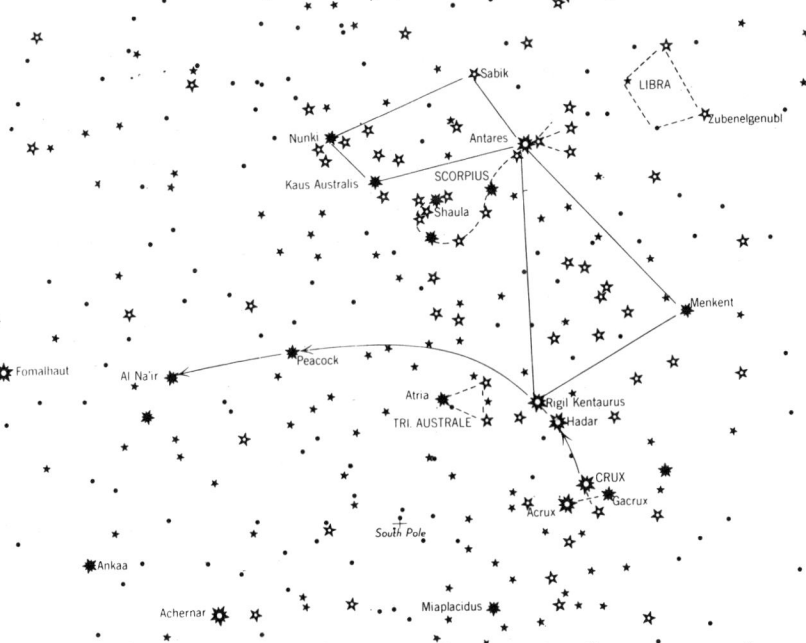

STARS IN THE VICINITY OF PEGASUS

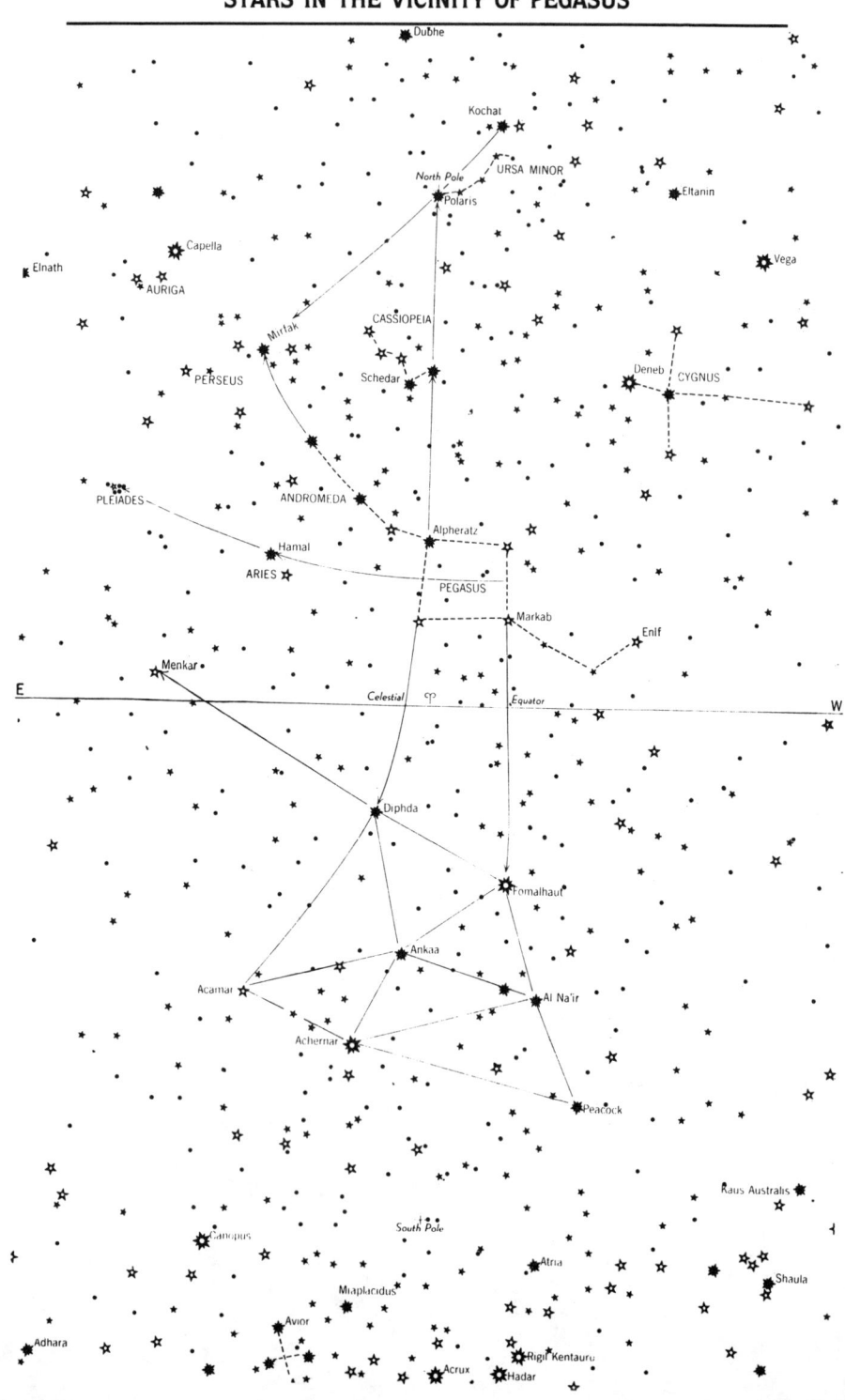

STARS IN THE VICINITY OF URSA MAJOR

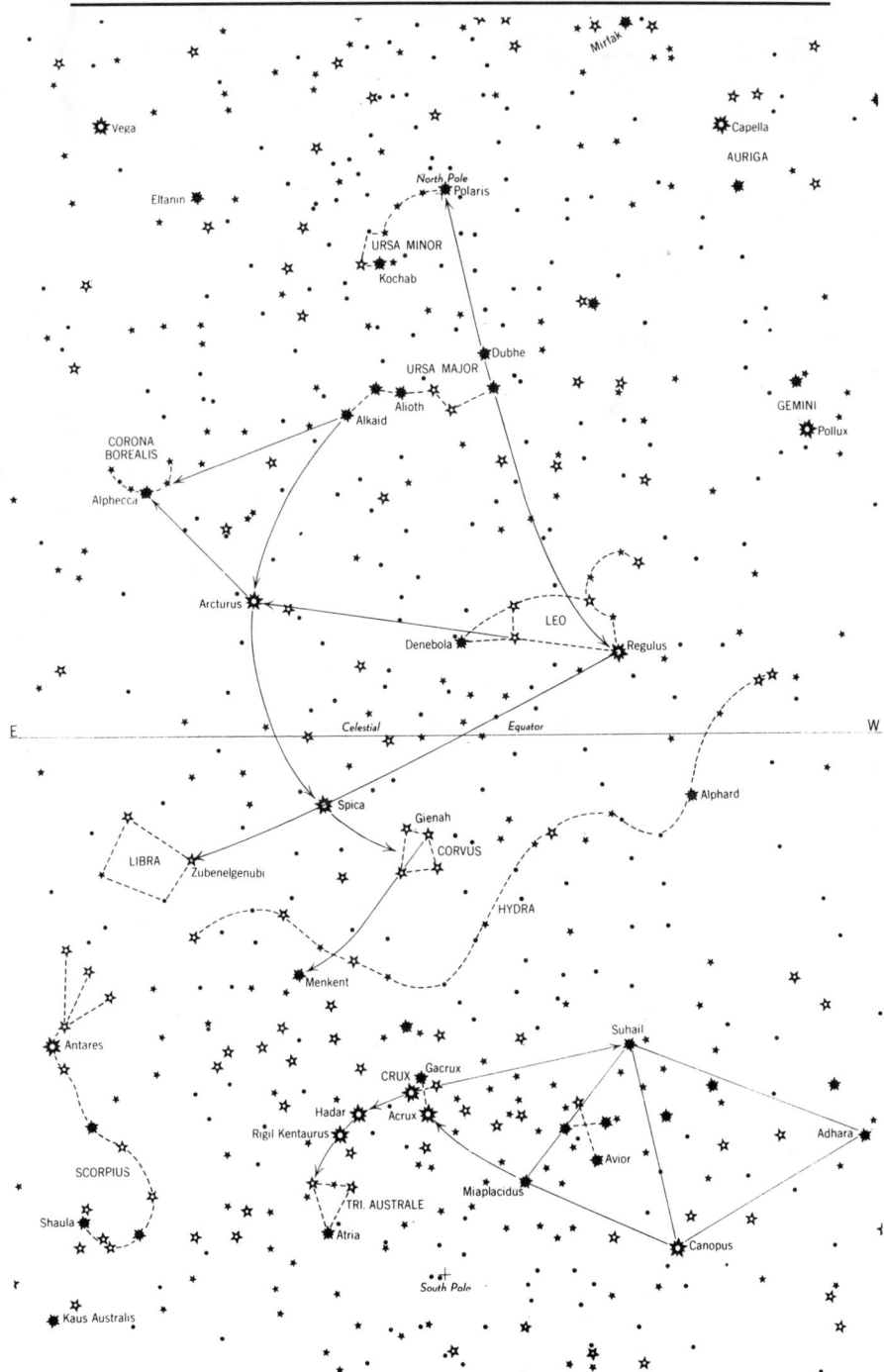

STARS IN THE VICINITY OF ORION

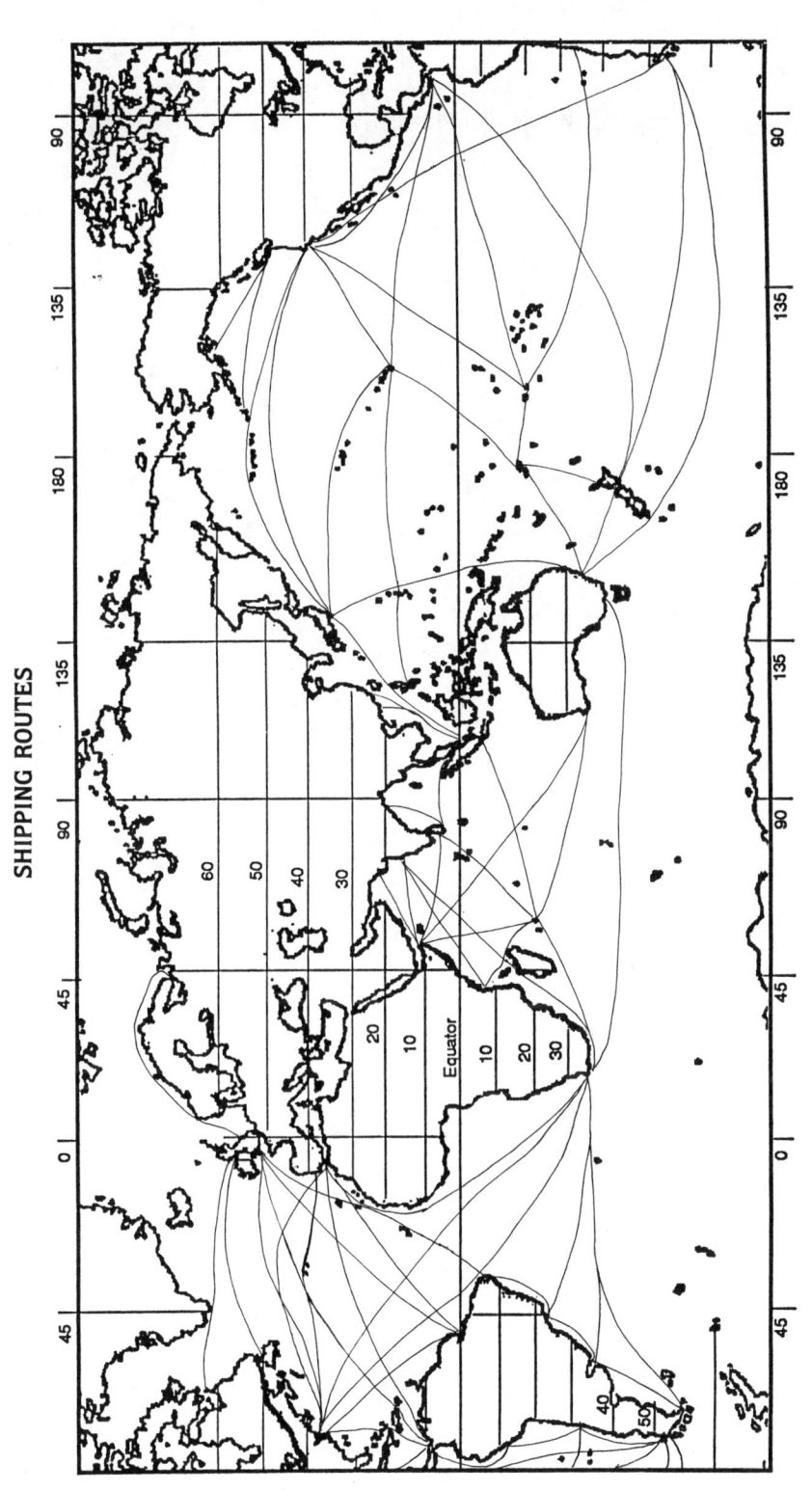

SHIPPING ROUTES

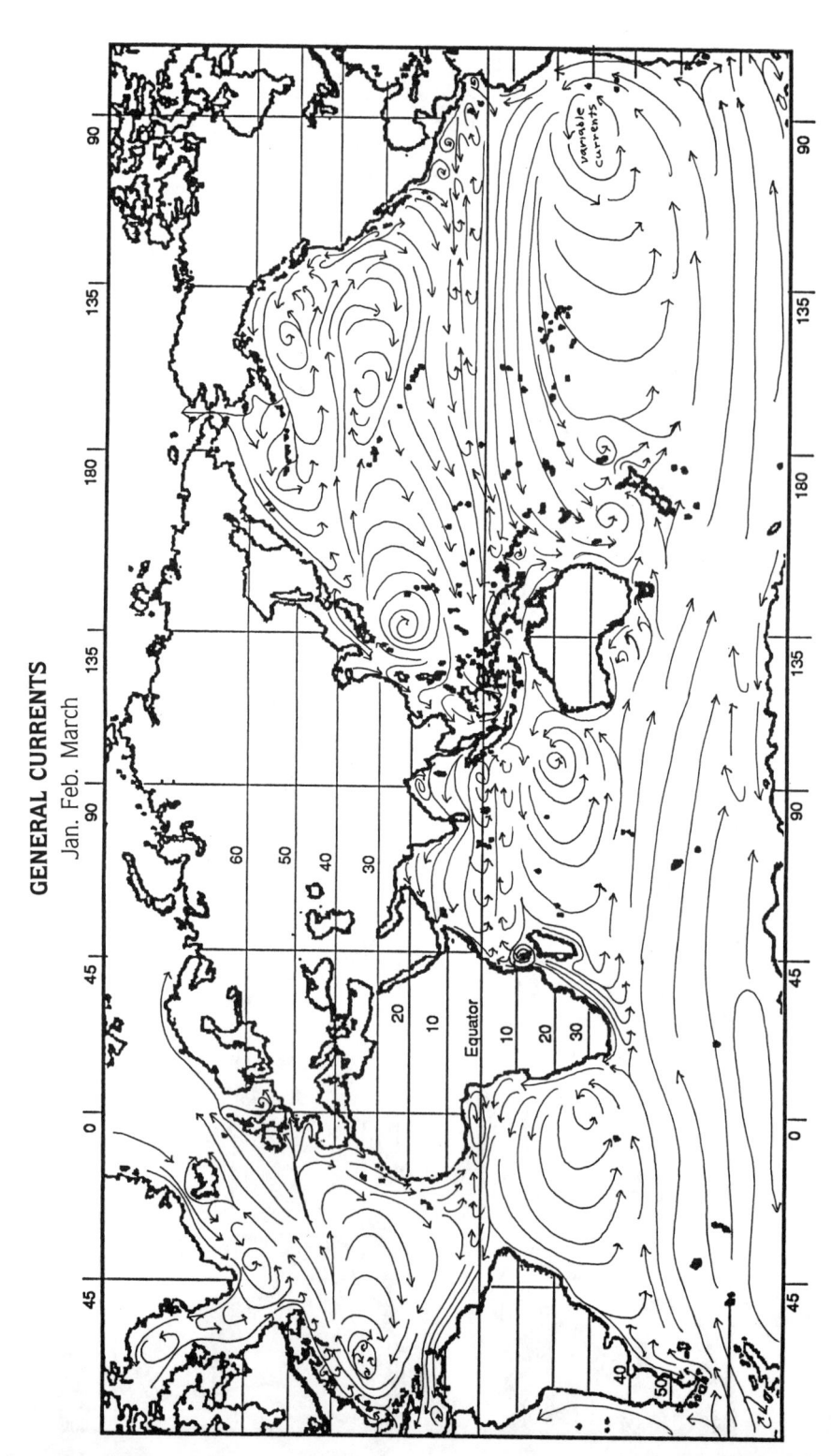

GENERAL CURRENTS
Jan. Feb. March

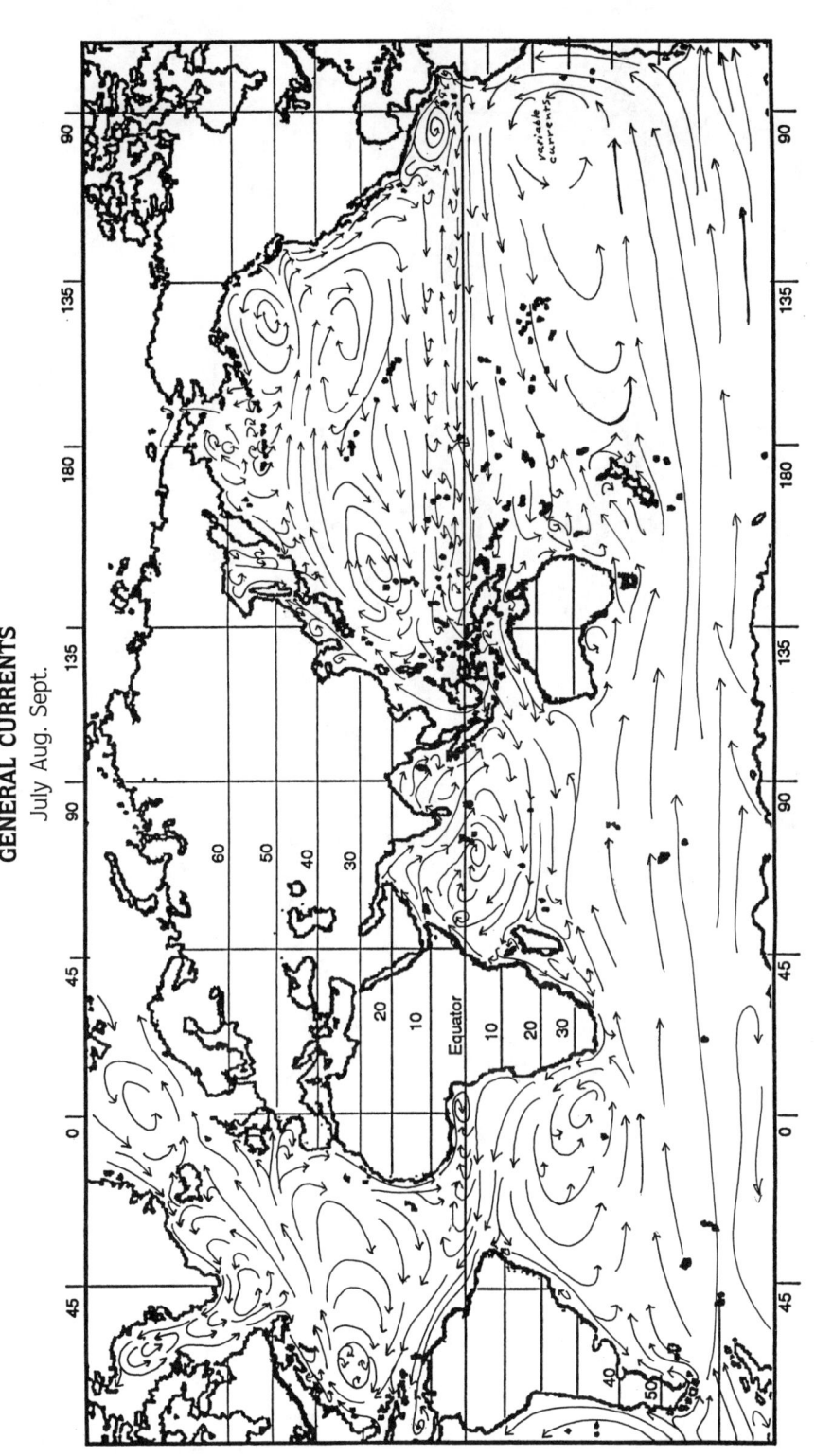

GENERAL CURRENTS
July Aug. Sept.

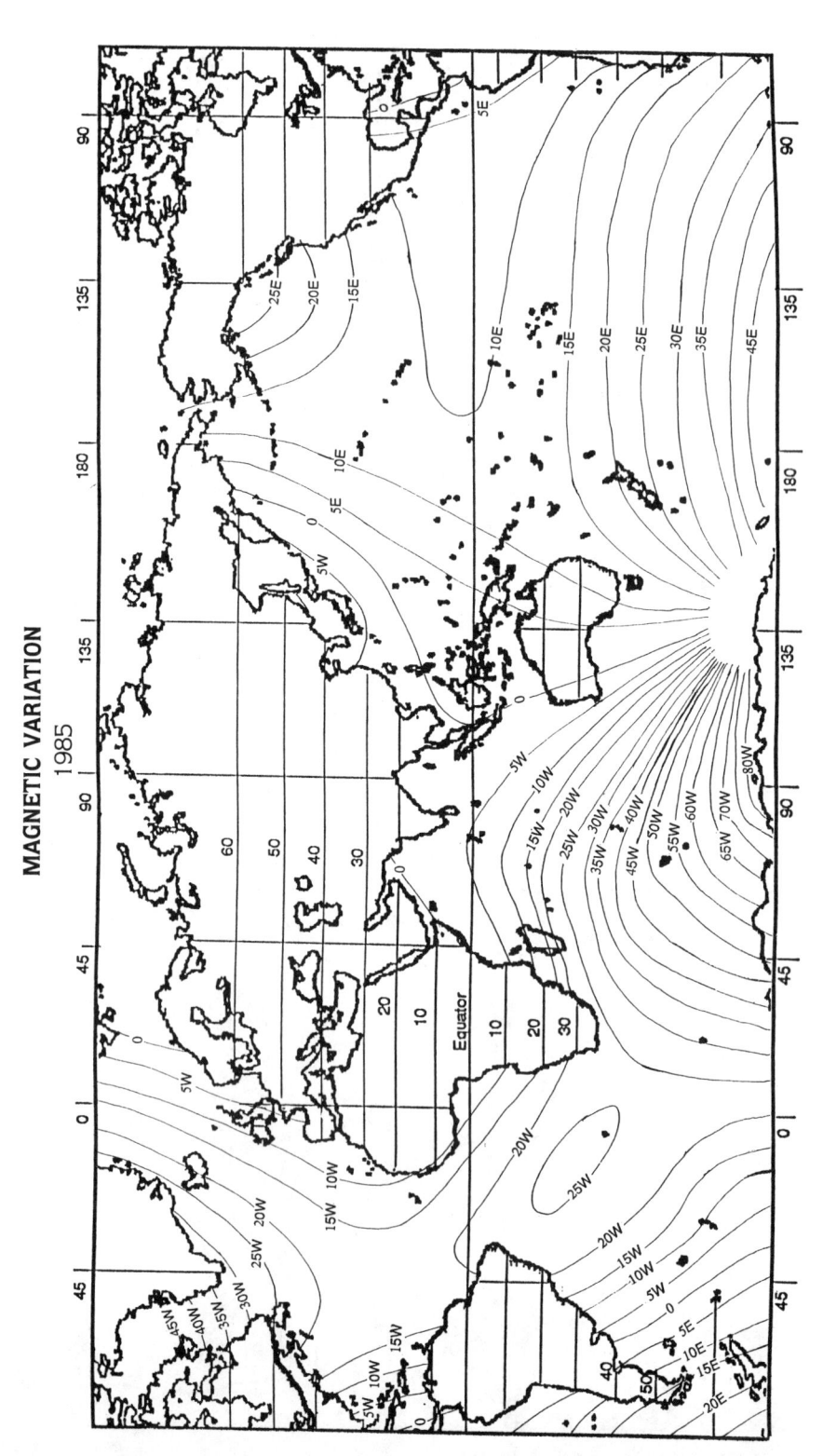

MAGNETIC VARIATION

1985

INDEX

The author would welcome comments or corrections for future editions of this book. Please write to:

Michael Cargal
3755 Avocado Boulevard, #512
La Mesa, CA 92041